DOLLARS & SENSE

Dennis V. Damp

Safe Investment Strategy

©

First edition

D-Amp Publications

Pittsburgh, PA.

DOLLARS & SENSE

Safe Investment Strategies

By Dennis V. Damp

PUBLISHED BY:

D-AMP Publications
401 Amherst Avenue
Coraopolis, Pa. 15108, USA

First Printing 1989

Printed in the United States of America

ISBN 0-943641-03-9

INTRODUCTION

Many investment books are written by professionals for professionals. The truly small investor, that doesn't have thousands in the bank and a $50,000 income, is virtually ignored by brokers and financial publications alike. The attitude is sink or swim.

Dennis Damp started investing in 1972 with $200 from his military discharge bonus. He found the investment world a hostile and unsympathetic environment.

After experiencing several losses he sought profitable and innovative ways to start investing on a shoe string budget. He discovered that many opportunities do exist for the small investor. Most aren't publicized . Primarily, stock brokers make a living on commission. If you can find a way to avoid paying commissions the broker loses and the small investor wins. Dennis realized that the sooner a savings program is initiated the greater gain realized and to increase total yield reduce or eliminate commissions whenever possible.

Dennis is an accomplished freelance writer that specializes in finances for the average american. His methods don't guarantee millions but suggest that you too can accumulate a sizable nestegg, in the hundreds of thousands, with as little as $25 per month and a small initial investment. This book was written to encourage the majority of Americans that they too can get a piece of the rock by investing a small sum in a safe investment regularly.

ACKNOWLEDGEMENT

I would like to thank the many contributors that supplied valuable research material, advice and interviews. Mr. Thomas O'hara, Chairman and Mr. Bruce Wagner, Director, Computer Operations for NAIC corp., Mr. John Reading from Value Line Inc., Mr Robert Atkinson, financial analyst for Equitable Resources Inc., The American Association of Individual Investors and to Evergreen Enterprises. A special thanks to Joy Vandenberg, Editor at Off Duty magazine, for her ability to work with writers to produce tight on target writing. Finally, without Dan Poynter's succinct guidance this book would not have been published.

I must also acknowledge another writer Bertha Pernisek Damp, my mother, who inspired and encouraged me throughout her short life, my son Dennis Jr. and daughter Sabrina who suffer through the long winters while dad works late hours in his home office. First and foremost I must thank my lifelong partner, wife, business manager and collaborator, Mary Damp. Without her support and encouragement none of this would have been possible.

TABLE OF CONTENTS

WARNING - DISCLAIMER

This book provides general investment information. It is sold with the understanding that the publisher and author are not engaged in rendering legal, investment advisory or other professional services. If expert assistance is needed, the services of a professional should be sought.

"Dollars And Sense" compliments, amplifies and supplements other texts. Additional references are interspersed throughout this book.

Dollars and Sense does not present a get rich quick scheme. To be a successful investor takes time and study. For many people, the investment programs offered in this book are affordable and build an educational foundation for future investment growth.

Every effort has been made to make this manual as complete and accurate as possible. However, there may be mistakes both typographical and in content. Therefore, this text should be used as a general guide and not as the ultimate source of investment information. Furthermore this book contains information on investing only up to the printing date.

This book's purpose is to educate new investors. The author and D-Amp Publications shall have neither liability nor responsibility to any person or entity with respect to any loss or damage caused or alleged to be caused directly or indirectly by the information contained in this book.

WARNING - DISCLAIMER

CHAPTER ONE

PRACTICAL / SAFE INVESTING

Financial security, money in the bank and a comfortable retirement is what dreams are made of. Your dreams can become reality with a little investment knowledge, common sense and personal initiative. Making millions overnight sounds great and books that promise it make authors and publishers rich. You won't make instant riches by following this books savings and investment programs. I would be highly suspicious of any such claims. If a million dollars could be made simply by reading one book everyone would be rich. What you can achieve are realistic savings and investment goals starting with as little as $25 per month. Maybe not millions, but Hundreds of Thousands accumulated through select investments and high powered savings programs. This won't happen overnight. The time tested investment programs presented in this book can produce dramatic results over time.

Stock market analysts, brokerage houses and financial magazines tend to confuse rather than untangle the investment menagerie that surrounds us. All wage earners should know how to safely take advantage of todays investment opportunities. I stress safety. Most, including myself, can't afford to jeopardize our families future by taking undo risks. It's easy to get caught up in the frenzy surrounding the stock market. Tips freely given seldom realize promised gains. Our parents told us " nothing is ever for free ". With investing this holds doubly true.

Discipline is the underlying theme of this book. Saving and investing regularly without fail achieves goals. I firmly believe in paying yourself first with every paycheck. Religiously put away your predetermined savings each pay - EVERY PAY - before you spend one red cent.

Time tested savings and investment principals are presented that provide basic knowledge and a foundation to build on with minimal risk. Risk taking should be left to those that know the ins and outs of the market and can make informed, intelligent investment decisions. With time and investment experience you too will be able to make informed decisions on higher risk investments. The higher the risk the greater potential reward. The best way to get your feet wet is by not getting them burnt. A gradual learning process through hands on investing is the surest and safest way to enter investments of any type.

When you first took driving lessons you began in an abandoned parking lot. Before starting the engine you got familiar with the car. When starting out your acceleration was uneven and your top speed a cautious twenty miles per hour. This book will provide slow, steady, and cautious acceleration, through investment knowledge and knowhow, and like becoming familiar with your first car you will become familiar with the financial world around you. At first driving was a frightening experience. So too is the investment world. By gradually getting onboard with the investment and savings programs offered you too will become familiar and comfortable with Safe Investment Strategies.

TAKING CHARGE

Remember the story about the investment advisor that bilked millions from his clients. Unscrupulous individuals are willing and quite able to fleece anyone that shows interest in their schemes. The only way to avoid this is to take charge of your own personal finances. A college education is not a prerequisite to understand the investment strategies presented in this book. A desire to learn, basic reading comprehension, and $25 per month is all that you will need to implement the programs offered.

There are between 150,000 to 500,000 Financial Planners that would be glad to take control for you. However, they generally work on a fee or percentage basis and prefer to manage minimum accounts of $100.000 or more. Fraud and abuse in the financial planning industry has resulted in a $400 million dollar loss for over 22,000 investors over the past two years according to the NASAA, North American Securities Administrators Association. To become a financial planner all you need do is file with the SEC, Securities and Exchange Commission. This involves filling out a standard form, sending $150 for registration and within 45 days you are registered "I.A.", Investment Advisor with the S.E.C.. Investment training or a financial background isn't required to register.

The majority of financial planners are honest hardworking individuals. Having a competent financial planner is no excuse for not knowing market basics. You wouldn't trust your car to a stranger yet many will put their entire life savings with someone they hardly know and give them total control.

If approached by a financial planner there are danger signals that should turn you off immediately to their proposals:

1. Offers guarantee unrealistic high yields such as 20% per year.

2. They won't explain investment plan details because it's to complex for the investor to understand.

3. Offers inside market information or an unusual sales pitch such as off shore banking or new exotic technology.

4. They aren't registered with state or federal regulators.

You have taken the first step to gain personal financial control by reading "Dollars and Sense ". On The Job Training (OJT) is a term used by the military. You will obtain investing OJT by beginning an investment and savings program that attracts your interest in this book. You can choose between No Load Mutual Funds, U.S. Treasury Securities, Savings Bonds, Certificates of Deposit, Money Market Accounts, IRA's, 401 K plans if available, and you will be able to buy stock direct from over 1,000 major companies and pay no sales commissions through numerous Dividend Reinvestment Programs. Lucrative savings hints are presented on how to avoid excessive interest on loans, pay off mortgages in half the time, and numerous tax saving tips all based on sound judgement and COMMON SENSE. After reading this book you will learn that a down market can be very good for the average small investor. In chapter two you will discover that you DO HAVE INVESTMENT CASH RIGHT NOW. Cash you never knew you had.

GETTING STARTED IS HALF THE BATTLE

Dynamic interplay , learning while doing, is the heart and soul of this book. As you read a chapter and collect additional information get involved and commit to a small investment and watch it grow. The earlier you start investing the greater the reward.

The table below presents the future value of $50 invested monthly at various interest rates and time periods. The interest is compounded quarterly. If you were to invest $50 monthly and received 12% interest on your investment you would have $37,566 in your account after 20 years and $185,851 in 35 years. You can use this table to determine what your investments would be worth for any multiple of $25. If you could save only $25 per month divide the dollar value in the chart columns by 2. In the example below, at 12% after after 20 years you would have one half of $37,566 or $18,783 by investing $25 per month. If $100 per month is invested multiply each columns dollar value by 2. Multiply $37,566 by 2 or you would have $75,132 in your account after 20 years had you invested $100 per month.

DOLLAR VALUE OF $50 DEPOSITED MONTHLY
AT VARIOUS INTEREST RATES AND YEARS
INTEREST COMPOUNDED QUARTERLY

Interest Rate	Years 10	20	35
8%	$ 9,128	$29,258	$113,228
10%	$10,194	$37,566	$185,851
12%	$11,422	$48,683	$311,523
15%	$13,608	$72,944	$696,995

We grow great by dreams. All big men are dreamers. They see things in the soft haze of a spring day or in the red fire of a long winter's evening. Some of us let these great dreams die, but others nourish and protect them, nurse them to the sunshine and light which come always to those who sincerely hope that their dreams will come true.

WOODROW WILSON

CHAPTER 2

YOUR HIDDEN ASSETS

Before determining what, when, and how to invest, evaluate your income, life-style, loans, credit card debts, savings and checking accounts to uncover hidden assets that can be used to start your plan. As little as $25 per month deposited into a 6% savings account will grow to $16,458 in 25 years. By investing in a mutual fund earning 12% annually the same $25 investment would grow to $39,900.

Why not let your pay check earn additional income for you. Many banks and savings institutions offer interest bearing checking accounts. By directly depositing your pay into an interest bearing checking account you can earn interest on your average daily balance. Some accounts compound interest daily. Check with local savings institutions to obtain the highest possible interest plus minimum monthly service charges. 5% annual interest on an average account balance of $1,000 would be $4.16 per month in earned interest. Over 12 months this would provide an additional $51 of income including compounded interest.

NOT MUCH YOU SAY!

The facts speak for themselves. THIS EXTRA $51 A YEAR, INVESTED AT A COMPOUNDED ANNUAL 8.0 PERCENT RATE WOULD BE WORTH $5,777.28 BEFORE TAXES IN 30 YEARS. Worth while? You be the judge.

The above example indicates just how powerful compounded interest is. You earn interest income on not only what you put into your account but on interest previously earned on your account balance. The following table will let you calculate how much your personal regular savings will grow over 5, 10, 20, and 30 year periods at various interest rates.

FUTURE ACCUMULATED VALUE OF $1 AT SEVERAL INTEREST RATES INTEREST IS COMPOUNDED ANNUALLY

Interest Rate	Years 5	10	20	30
6%	5.64	13.18	36.79	79.06
8%	5.87	14.49	45.76	113.28
10%	6.11	15.94	52.27	164.49
12%	6.35	17.55	72.05	241.33
14%	6.61	19.34	91.03	356.79
16%	6.88	21.32	115.38	530.31

Determine how much you can afford to save yearly. With $50 per month, $600 per year, at 10% interest you would have $98,694 (164.49 x $600) saved in 30 years. Follow the estimated annual percentage rate, 10% in this example, across the chart until you arrive at the 30 year column. Multiply 164.49, found under the 30 year column, times your estimated yearly savings amount. The result will be your accounts value for the years selected.

The above chart is for interest compounded annually. Savings and investment programs compound interest semiannually, quarterly, monthly or daily. Compounding determines how often you earn interest on your savings. The shorter the compounding interval the more you earn. With the chart above your interest earned, called yield, is the same throughout the year. When interest compounds more frequently than annually the effective yield increases and savings grow faster. If you placed $50.00 per month into an investment earning %10 compounded monthly you would have $113,024.40 in thirty years and your effective yield would be 10.47%. Look for the highest interest with the shortest compounding period to increase your interest income.

Loans and credit card interest payments can be cut dramatically. Credit card companies typically charge between 18% and 21% interest. If your credit card bills amount to $2000.00 at 21% interest you will pay $466.54 total interest over two years. By refinancing through a credit union or bank loan at 10.5% you would pay only $226.05 interest saving $240.49 in interest payments. occasionally, banks offer discount loan programs below market rates to entice new customers. Not long ago I obtained a 9.9% loan when all other banks in my area were offering 11% or more.

Bank savings accounts now earn a meager 5 to 5.5 percent interest. If you have over $1,000 in your savings account consider shifting a portion of your savings to a Certificate of deposit that can pay several percentage points higher interest. If you can't afford to tie up your cash for 3 months or longer in a CD consider shifting a portion of your savings into a higher interest rate money market account. Money market accounts typically pay higher interest compounded daily and have check writing privileges. Certificates of Deposit and Money Market accounts are discussed in greater detail in chapter 3. Banks and stock brokerage firms offer insured money market accounts. Money market accounts generally require an initial deposit of between $50 to several thousand dollars. Look for the lowest initial deposit and best interest rate.

The interest bearing checking account, loan refinancing, and increased savings account income would have conservatively provided $15 per month, in the examples given, that could be used for investing. This came strictly from cost cutting and not from digging deeper into your pockets. You can make profitable changes in your life and substantially increase this amount.

Cigarettes cost around $10.00 per carton or 94 cents per pack. I'm not suggesting you entirely quite smoking if that's what you truly want to do. What I suggest is cut your smoking in half. If you have a two pack a day habit, you not only would put away approximately $28 per month in a profitable adventure but you could improve your health at the same time.

Secondly, how about a packed lunch? You can pack a lunch for a dollar a day. If you normally spend $3.50 for lunch that's a 2.50 savings or $50.00 per month. How about buying generic food products instead of name brands. Coupon cutting can cut hundreds of dollars from your yearly food bill.

Reduce insurance premiums by requesting competitive quotes from several insurance agents. A friend was paying, what I considered to be, very high auto insurance premiums. His coverage, cars owned and number of drivers was similar to mine, yet he was paying $2600 per year for the same coverage I received for $1,000. By shopping around he cut over $600 off of his premiums without reducing coverage. We attributed the $1,000 difference in premiums to commuting distance. His daily commute to work was 50 miles round trip while mine was less than 4 miles.

Home owners insurance premiums also differ dramatically from agency to agency. Recently I switched companies saving over $20 per year in premiums, increased my coverage by $25,000 and added water damage coverage for sewer backup and pipe breakage that I did not have on my old policy.

A little soul searching on your part will uncover many areas that are potential money makers. Now that we have the resources we must develop an investment strategy. The remaining chapters present a low risk and profitable way to begin investing and will put your investment and savings goals on track.

CHAPTER 3

INVESTMENT FUNDAMENTALS

The investment community thrives on key phrases and catch words that create undue fear for the average investor; Annuity, appreciation, option trading, puts, calls, book value, and PE ratios, are market terms you may hear frequently. If you served in the military or work for a government agency they too have their own vernacular simplified with a thousand acronyms. The investment terms used in this book will be fully explained when first encountered. See chapter 11 for a glossary of common investment terms.

INVESTMENT GOALS

There are three prime considerations you must take into account before making your first investment, SAFETY OF

PRINCIPAL, INCOME, AND GROWTH. Each goal is tied to what you intend to gain from your investments and where you are at in life.

Individuals over fifty must rank safety number one to preserve their capital for retirement. Younger investors may be willing to assume higher risks to achieve greater gains from their investments. Greater gains often mean greater risk. With risk is the potential of loss of principal at least for the short term. The younger investor can ride out a bear market, a market where the economy is depressed and stock prices down, and wait for stock prices to return to high levels. Middle age investors generally take moderate risks with a portion of their investment dollars while placing the rest into safe income producing investments.

This book will concentrate on safety, income and preservation of your investment dollars. Until you are comfortable with investing and know how the market functions SAFETY COMES FIRST. There is nothing more discouraging than first investing in a hot tip stock only to watch it's price fall to a fraction of its purchased price.

SAFETY OF PRINCIPAL

Most investors have funds set aside for know urgent needs. College education, retirement funds, savings for a new home, etc.. These funds are generally placed in government bonds, certificates of deposit or money market funds. The principal, dollars invested, is not subject to change with the economy or circumstance. You will generally receive a return, interest earned, that meets or exceeds the inflation rate.

INCOME

Income producing investments are used to supplement your current income or to augment retirement and social security payments. Interest or dividends provide a return or yield. Yield is the percentage of yearly gain received on your money. If you earn $100 on a $1000 investment your yield is 10%. You can calculate yield by dividing the yearly dividends received by the current stock price and multiplying the result by 100. In the example above this would be $100/$1000 X 100 = 10%. Return - is expressed in dollars and would be $100. The yield lets you compare investments. The higher the yield the more income you generate. High yields are generally higher risk investments. There is a trade off made for very high rates of return. That trade off is the risk you incur to your investment dollars.

Many companies pay out dividends on their stock. Dividends are expressed as a yield in relation to the companies stock price. If a stock sells for $20 per share and pays a $1.00 dividend the yield is 5%. You would receive 25c each quarter, every three months, for each share owned.

Yield can change daily with stock price fluctuations. If the stock goes up to $30 per share the return is still $1.00. The yield reduced to 3.3%. The reduced yield is only for those that purchased the stock at $30 per share. If you had purchased the stock at $20 per share your yield is still 5%.

GROWTH

When you purchased the stock in the example above at $20.00 per share and then it increased in value to $30.00 the increased price appreciation is the growth, growth of capital or a capital gain of $10 per share. If you sold at $30 your capital gains would be 50% plus you would have realized quarterly dividend income if the stock was held for more than three months. Capital or capitalization represents the total dollar value of a stock or company. Growth of capital is the greatest advantage of common stock investing.

Growth stocks generally offer a low yield and in many cases no yield at all. Investors purchase stocks that have the potential for growth to realize substantial gains over their initial investment. The ideal situation is to find a blue chip, high quality, company that has a fair dividend yield plus has potential for increased price appreciation, capital gains. In bear markets many blue chips have average to high yields. That's why you hear that safe money is in blue chips. Even if an individual had purchased a quality stock in a bull market, the economy is strong and investor confidence high, and a recession occurs the investor, if he or she holds their investment long enough, will get a fair yield and the price will eventually return to its former level.

MARKET DYNAMICS

It is important to realize how the market cycles, changes from bull to bear. The market is constantly changing. Economic and political news and events influences prices and investor confidence. The market swings naturally from highs to lows and back to highs as time progresses. Generally the smart knowledgeable investors are selling in a bull market, prices rising, to realize capital gains. You only realize capital gains if you sell. The stock market anticipates trends months in advance of when the event actually occurs. The average investor is swayed more by the excitement of the market than it's reality. The majority of small investors hold off buying until they see a definite upward trend then wait until the pace gets frenzied. This is when the market is hitting new highs weekly and the stock market is in the news daily.

When times are good we all want to get on the band wagon. Unfortunately, the market becomes oversold, stock values becomes over inflated, and the market reverses. The smart money got out on the way to the top, the average investor buys in all the excitement then sees their investment diminish in value dramatically overnight.

No one truly knows exactly when this reversal is about to happen. There are too many variables in the equation. Tell tale signs, flags signaling the end of a bull or bear market, appear that warn the informed investor. Astute professional investors spend their entire life studying the market and take calculated risks based on their experience. The average investor doesn't have the exorbitant time needed to analyze market fundamentals. Yet an average investor can succeed by following three key guide lines.

1) BUY WHEN THE MARKET IS DEPRESSED (stock prices low)

2) DOLLAR COST AVERAGE

3) DIVERSIFICATION

Everyone tells you to BUY LOW AND SELL HIGH to be successful. Sure! it makes sense to the most casual observer. It's not as simple as it sounds. You have to break some major psychological barriers to subscribe to a buy low theory.

How easy would it be to buy when everyone and your uncle is telling you that the worst is yet to happen. In the depth of a bear market the majority of analysts are discouraged about market performance and indicators. The doomsday soothsayers come out of the woodwork telling us the market will never recover and that the GREAT DEPRESSION is returning. It's a psychological game that's played on both sides of the market cycle. During a bull market most analysts don't see the precipitous cliff up ahead. The market has been good to them and they see nothing but blue skys and bright sunshine ahead. BUY-BUY-BUY.

You must buy when prices are depressed. This doesn't mean to buy only during a recession. Certain industries are out of favor at various times for one reason or another. You need to look for quality companies that will come out of the slump swinging and healthy. The following chapters will help you make those decisions.

Dollar cost averaging is the second tool. This is the principle of investing at regular intervals no matter what the market is doing. When the market is low, depressed prices, you put in the same predetermined amount, better yet increase your regular investment if possible, to buy more shares at depressed prices. When the market is high you continue to contribute your predetermined amount at regular intervals. This averages your cost per share over time. If you purchased $50 worth of stock selling for $5 per share you would buy 10 shares. The next month the stock rose to $6 per share and you purchased $50 worth and received 8.333 shares. You now have 18.88 shares that your average price per share is now $100 divided by 18.33 or $5.45 per share.

With this method your average price per share never reaches the actual high price per share. This approach takes discipline. Again when the market is depressed it's easy to forego sending in your regular monthly investment. When the market gets hot you start up again. This defeats the benefits of dollar cost averaging.

Mutual funds will debit your savings or checking account monthly. This is the best way to insure you keep up with the program. When the market is depressed, send more if you can afford to.

Diversification is simply spreading your risk by not investing all of your funds in one or two investments. A well diversified investment program would divide your investments into several categories;

1) Insured money market accounts or CD's
2) U.S. EE Savings Bonds or Treasuries
3) IRA's or 401k retirement accounts
4) Mutual funds of various types
5) Individual stocks through dividend reinvestment plans

This concept is considered the ultimate factor in protecting your assets. Diversification is even practiced within each of the above categories. Mutual funds can be purchased to satisfy any investment appetite. From highly speculative to ultra conservative. Stocks from different industry groups help to balance your portfolio. (A portfolio is your personal investment collection of stocks, bonds, mutual funds, etc.) When one industry is down another is experiencing phenomenal growth. One offsets the other and your total investment package's net worth tends to average out.

Initially your funds will be limited. Begin slowly with one investment. As time passes and your accounts grow you can then begin a total diversification program. Mutual funds, as explained later, are highly diversified to begin with.

TYPES OF INVESTMENTS

The following list is not all inclusive. Their are literally hundreds of investment vehicles available today. This list compliments the following chapters. As you gain market insight and knowledge you may wish to expand into other higher risk investments.

COMMON STOCK

Corporations issue stock and can own property in its own name. If a company issued 100,000 shares and you purchased 1,000 shares you would own 1% of the company. Two types of stock are generally issued, common and preferred.

SHAREHOLDERS RIGHTS

A. the right to sell your shares;
B. the right to receive dividends when authorized by the

the company;
C. the right to attend shareholder meetings;
D. the right to receive a share of a companies assets if dissolved;
E. the right to review certain company books;
F. the right to attend the companies annual meetings and receive annual reports;
G. the right to vote for company directors;
H. the right of limited liability;

Preferred stock holders have first claim on company assets after creditors during bankruptcy proceedings. Common stock owners receive the remaining assets left after the creditors have been paid and the preferred stock owners satisfied.

Common stock permits individuals to participate in company growth. When assets and income increase stock value increases along with dividend payouts. You can realize significant capital gains from stock investments. Sears stock sold for $57 per share in 1906. 100 shares purchased at $5,700 then would be worth over $2 million today. Common stock prices have increased steadily over the past century. Stocks are excellent long term investments that guard against inflation. This is true for strong, well managed companies. Citicorp has paid dividends continuously since 1813 and over the past several years have increased dividends 10% a year. Four other companies have paid dividends even longer.

BONDS

A bond is a debt instrument. The company or governmental agency that issues a bond promises to pay a stated interest amount at specified intervals for a predetermined time period. A 30 year bond will pay its stated interest direct to the bond holder for thirty years. After thirty years the company will return the face amount of the bond to the owner. Bonds are one of the safest investments plus offer secure income. This holds true only for high rated corporate and government bonds. There are what the industry refers to as JUNK bonds, low rating and safety, available. They offer higher interest but are more susceptible to default.

Zero coupon bonds sell at a discount, below face value, similar to E E Savings bonds. No interest payments are made for the term of the bond. After holding the bond to maturity you will receive the full face value.

Debentures are bonds but differ in one respect. They aren't secured by the company's assets only earnings.

Bonds are excellent investments if you can hold them to maturity. If you need to cash them in you must sell them on a secondary bond market. Bonds are rate sensitive. This means if interest rates go up, above the interest rate being paid on your bond, the selling price of your bond on the secondary market will be less than what you paid. Investors could buy bonds at the higher interest rate and to be competitive the face value of your bond would decrease to provide a comparable yield.

SAVINGS BONDS

Series EE Savings Bonds, ideal for small investors, are one of the safest investment you can make. There is no charge or commission to the purchaser. Savings bonds are sold at a 50% discount from the stated face value. A $50 bond sells for $25. Bonds can be purchased in denominations from $50 to $10,000 with a yearly limit of $30,000 face value ($15,000 discount). When your bond matures you receive full face value.

The interest rate is determined twice each year in May and November. 7.35% is the current rate. This rate varies at 85% of the average 5 year Treasury Securities yield over the past six months. If you cash your bond in within the first five years you will not receive this rate. The rate of return will range from 4.16% up to the current rate.

Federal taxes on savings bond interest earned is tax deferred until they mature or are cashed. States and local municipalities do not tax savings bond interest. When bonds mature you can roll them over into HH bonds to defer taxes. HH bonds pay monthly interest payments to the owner. You can purchase savings bonds through payroll deduction, at banks, savings and loans, credit unions or through your local Federal Reserve Bank. Savings Bonds can be purchase through the mail by writing to the Bureau of Public Debt, EE Savings Bonds, Parkersburg, WV 26106-1328.

MONEY MARKET DEPOSIT ACCOUNTS

Money market accounts are offered by banks and mutual funds and have competitive interest rates, rates higher than standard passbook savings. Mutual fund accounts typically offer a higher yield than banks, about 1% higher. Bank accounts are guaranteed by the FDIC, Federal Deposit Insurance Corporation, for up to $100,000 while mutual fund accounts are not insured.

A minimum investment of between $50 and several thousand dollars is required to open an account. After your account is opened your balance can fall below the minimum initial investment. When this happens your interest earned decreases or a monthly service charge is applied.

You are permitted to write up to three checks per month on your money market account assets. Withdrawals from your account are also permitted. The total number of monthly transactions are limited by the financial institution and Federal regulations. If your savings account is over $1,000 it would pay you to close it and open a money market account.

CERTIFICATES OF DEPOSIT

A Certificate of Deposit is a debt instrument offered by all financial institutions similar to a bond issue. The bank quaranties it will pay you a set interest for a predetermined time period. Six month and one, two, three and five year certificates are common. Yields vary from one institution to another. Many local papers publish weekly lists of CD rates for all local financial institutions. Shop around for the best rate. CD's are guaranteed by the issuing bank or savings and loan for up to $100,000.

It's difficult to compare yields on CD's. Financial institution calculate yield differently depending on compounding periods, reinvested earned interest, etc.. To avoid the confusion ask each bank officer how much you will have after one year. Also, early withdrawal penalties vary. You stand to loose 3 to 6 months interest with an early withdrawal. Look for the highest dollar return and lowest interest penalty.

CD's can be purchased from stock brokers. These too are insured by the issuing bank. You do not pay an early withdrawal penalty when purchasing and trading CD's from a stock broker. You will pay a sales and purchase commission for each transaction. Ask your broker which bank issued the certificate. You must make sure the bank is insured and on a safe financial footing.

If you feel that interest rates have peaked and are on a down trend you would want to purchase a longer term CD to protest your earned interest. If rates are on the increase you would purchase a short term 3 month CD in the hopes that after three months rates would rise to a more favorable level. Don't get too greedy. Five years ago when rates were 14% many of my associates opted for short term 1 year CD's thinking rates were going to 16 or 18%. One year later they were down to 11% and all wished they had opted for 5 year certificates.

TREASURY BILLS,NOTES and BONDS

U.S Treasuries are safe investments that pay competitive rates. They can be purchased form most banks, Federal reserve Banks, stock brokers, or direct from the Bureau of Public Debt. You must pay Federal tax on earned Interest, however interest is exempt from state and local taxes.

Treasury Bonds mature in 10 to 30 years. You must invest a minimum of $1,000. Bills mature in much shorter intervals of 13, 26 or 52 weeks. Treasury Bills sell below face value. This is called the discount. Treasury Bills are redeemed at face value upon maturity. Minimum investments are high, $10,000.

Treasury Notes mature in 1 to 10 years and pay a fixed rate. Interest is paid out twice a year. A $5,000 minimum investment is required for maturities under four years and $1,000 minimum for maturities of 4 years or more. A secondary market exists that will trade your Notes before the maturity date if you have to sell them.

MUTUAL FUNDS

Mutual funds are professionally managed investment companies. Their objective is to pool investors cash to purchase stocks, bonds, U.S. Treasuries and other assets to earn profit for the shareholders. Their are over 230 funds to choose from. Funds are divided into groups with common investment goals. Their are growth, Income, money market, bond, sector, equity, balanced and total return funds available. This is only a partial list.

Their are two groupings, load and no-load funds. A load is a sales commission. Chapter five will explain mutual funds in detail and concentrate on no-load funds to maximize your returns.

DIVIDEND REINVESTMENT PLANS

You can purchase stock direct from over 1000 major corporations commission free and automatically reinvest dividends quarterly. Most plans allow additional cash investments. No stock broker commissions are paid when you make additional purchases. Many companies offer a discount of up to 10% when you opt to reinvest your dividends. A T & T, Quaker Oats, and Mc Donalds Corporation are examples of the quality stocks that offer lucrative plans. Chapter six explains how Dividend Reinvestment Plans function and shows you how to get on board with your own personal program. These programs allow the average investor to buy fractions of a share and send in as little as $10 to make additional purchases.

THE FIRST STEP

It can be difficult deciding on what to invest in first. All investments have both benefits and disadvantages. The following chapters will help to clarify these points. After careful consideration of your financial position you too will be able to make a rational decision. No matter what you decide, take that giant leap and GET STARTED INVESTING. Your future may depend on it.

This chapter is an introduction to and not a comprehensive presentation or study of market fundamentals. Information presented is meant to provide the reader with an overview of market dynamics.

After you begin investing you will more than likely want additional information. There are excellent sources available at reasonable to no cost. Each following chapter will build on what you now know. Additional fundamental market characteristic are presented that complement each chapter. Appendix A lists sources for additional valuable investment information.

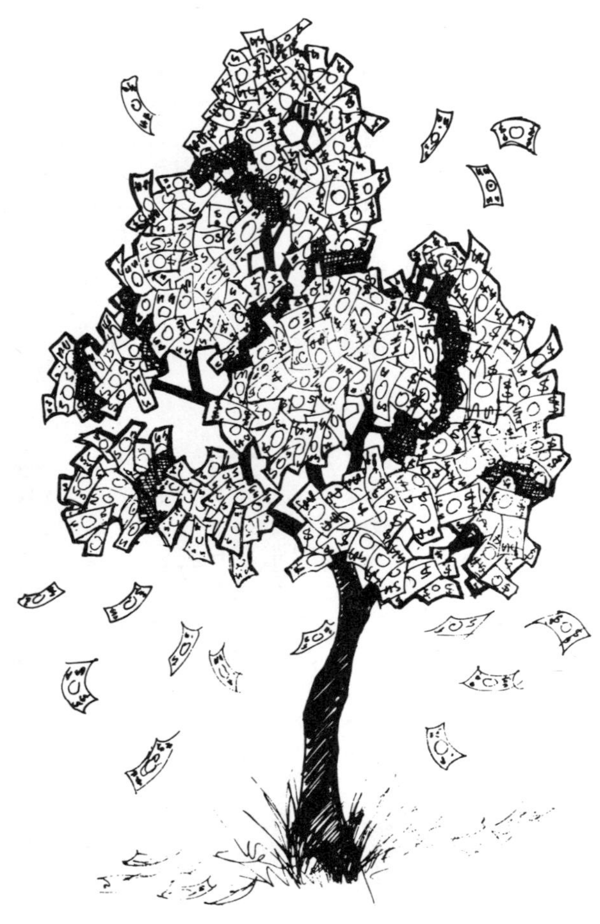

CHAPTER 4

READING THE FINANCIAL PAGES

To track your investments you must be able to read and understand stock listings on the New York, American and Over The Counter exchanges. You will also want to follow your mutual fund daily. Most newspapers print stock listings for at least the New York Exchange. Partial AMEX, American Stock Exchange, and OTC, Over the Counter, lists are available in the same paper. Comprehensive listings are printed daily in the Wall Street Journal or the Investors Daily publication. U.S.A. Today has an excellent Money section listings thousands of stocks and mutual funds.

TYPICAL NY STOCK EXCHANGE LISTING

NYSE QUOTES 10/7/88

New York Stock Exchange Issues

52 week High	Low	Stock	Div	Yld	PE	Sales 100's	High	Low	Last	Chg.
					A					
....										
....										
8 3/8	10 5/8	AMI	.72	4.1	14	x2110	17 5/8	17 1/4	17 5/8	+3/8
....										
....										
....										
....										
76 7/8	41 1/2	AmStor	.84	1.5	15	128	56 5/8	56 1/8	56 1/2	---
83 1/4	51	A Str pfA	4.38	7.0	15	63	63 1/4	62 1/4	62 1/4	-3/4
34 3/8	23	AT & T	1.20	4.5	14	8731	26 1/2	26 1/4	26 3/8	---
20 1/8	13 7/8	AmWtr	.68	3.8	10	779	18 1/4	17 7/8	18 1/8	+1/2
14 1/4	8 1/4	AmHotl	---	---	58	1425	13 7/8	13 7/8	13 7/8	+1/8
....										
....										
....										
					D					
....										
....										
....										
....										
79 3/4	41 1/4	Disney	.40	.6	17	1931	64 3/4	64 1/4	64 1/4	-3/8
5 3/4	3 1/8	Divrsin	---	---	--	29	4 3/8	4 1/4	4 3/8	-1/8
47 1/4	36 5/8	DomRs	3.08	7.0	10	790	43 3/4	43 1/2	43 3/4	+1/4
....										
....										
....										

TERMS

52 week high - The highest selling price over the past year.

52 week low - The lowest selling price over the past year.

Look down the lists in your daily paper. You will be surprised at how many stocks had significant price spreads. A spread is the difference between historical high and low selling prices. This indicates stock volatility. Because of BLACK MONDAY many stocks have significant spreads over the past year.

Stock - An abbreviation assigned to each listed stock. American Telegraph and Telephone is abbreviated A T & T.

Div Yld - "Dividend Yield" A percentage indicating the return on your investment that is received from dividend payments. If a stock sells for $20 per share and pays out $1.00 per year the yield is 5%.

PE - "Price to Earnings ratio" The price of a stock divided by its earnings per share. When a stock sells for $10 per share and the company earns income of $1.00 per share the PE would be 10. Generally the lower the PE the better quality stock. Each industry group sells within standard PE ranges. High tech stocks have a very high PE ratio. Companies that do not list a PE had a loss for the year or had insignificant , very low, earnings.

Sales in 100's- The number of stock shares sold the previous day in units of a hundred. Stocks are generally sold in even lots. An even lot is equal to 100 shares. An odd lot transaction is any purchase of less than 100 shares. With a listing of 78 sales in 100's add two zeros to calculate the total stock traded that day or 7800 shares in this example. The number of shares traded is an indicator of market interest. High volume indicates many traders are moving into and out of an issue. High volume on decreasing price movement indicates more people are selling the issue than are buying and viceversa. High volume is relative to company capitalization, (total stocks outstanding). What may appear as very high volume may in fact be a very small percentage of total shares outstanding. AT & T appears to be very active. However, there are over 246,000,000 shares outstanding. 780,000 shares of AT & T stock sold in one day represents less that .3% of the total shares outstanding. With a company having 10,000,000 shares outstanding 780,000 shares traded in one day would represent 7.8% of the companies total capitalization. 7.8% is considerable volume for any company to trade in one day.

High and Low - The preceding days high and low price paid per share. This indicates daily movement. A large spread or daily increasing spread indicates interest and activity that day. Point and figure chart analysts plot price moves in 1/8ths of a point (1 point equals $1 - and 1/8 point equals 12 1/2 cents). These analysts look for price trend lines to establish and use daily price movement to determine when to sell and buy.

last - This indicates what the last trade sold for that day. It tells an investor in which direction his stock was headed within the daily spread.

Chg - The increase or decrease in stock price from one day to the next expressed in fractions of a share. A - 1/8th indicates that your stock fell 12 1/2 cents from the previous days selling price. A 1 1/2 indicates your stock sold for $1.50 more yesterday than the day before.

Footnotes provide additional information. If you look at the above NYSE listing for AMI you will notice an "x" to the left of the sales figure. This x indicates that AMI Corporation declared a dividend on that date to all shareholders of record. A "u" indicates a new 52 week, price per share, high had been reached and "d" denotes a new 52 week low. Look for the footnote section in your papers financial section for a complete explanation of abbreviations used.

Many newspapers print only the stock name, closing sales price and change. The Wall Street Journal prints the Bid and Ask column for the NASDAQ or OTC, Over The Counter Exchange. The difference between the bid and ask price is the sales commission you must pay. The difference is often 1/8th of a point or 12 1/2 cents per share. You always pay the higher of the two quoted prices to purchase these shares.

Mutual funds list the fund, sell, buy and change column. See table 4-1.

TABLE 4-1

MUTUAL FUNDS

Closing Quotations

Fund	Sell	Buy	Chg
VALUE LINE FD:			
Aggrin	8.08	NL	---
Conv	10.78	NL	.02
Fund	13.34	NL	+.01
Incom	5.85	NL	---
Lev Gt	18.81	NL	+.03
MunBd	10.26	NL	---
Spl Sit	11.34	NL	+.01
US Gvt	11.81	NL	---
Van Eck:			
GldRs p	4.59	4.96	+.06
Intinv	11.40	12.46	+.12
Wldin p	9.37	10.13	+.02
WldTr p	12.83	13.87	-.01

....
....
....
....

The following footnotes are used by U.S.A. Today for their Mutual Fund listings.

NL - "No Load" indicates that this fund does not charge a sales commission. The buy and sell price is the same.

e - "capital gains distribution previous day". Mutual funds must pay out their capital gains, gains received from the sale of securities held by the fund, at least annually. Unlike owning individual stock, you realize capital gains even though you did not sell your shares in the fund.

p - "12-b1 fee". A 12-b1 fee is charged by many funds to cover promotional and other operating expenses. Locate a fund that does not access 12-b1 charges. Many funds charge 12-b1 expenses. There are over 300 no load funds that DO NOT. You want to put all of your money to work for you right away. Loads - sales commissions - and 12-b1 expenses can take as much as 10% of you initial investment and in some cases even more.

x - A cash dividend was paid the previous day. Growth and Income funds often pay dividends and capital gains.

Many excellent magazines offer good sound financial advice and explain the many facets of the market. MONEY Magazine, Consumer Reports and Changing Times all feature investment articles for the novice investor. Money Magazine provides helpful savings, investing, and tax planning strategies along with successful Retirement planning. Now that your investment knowledge is growing, you will find their articles more thought provoking.

This chapter exposed you to what you must know for the succeeding Chapters. As you mature as an investor you may get involved with higher risk investing and wish to learn more about other investment alternatives.

THere are two times in
a man's life when he
should not speculate -
when he cannot afford it,
and when he can.

Mark Twain

INFLATION

The reason we don't have inflation or unemployment in Austria is, we've exported all our economists to the United States and Canada.

Anonymous Austrian Diplomat

CHAPTER 5

MUTUAL FUND INVESTING

On October 19, 1987, BLACK MONDAY, the stock market crashed. Mutual funds lost 6% of their value according to ICI, the Investment Company Institute, while stocks fell 25 % during the same period. Conservative balanced mutual funds diversify to protect your investment. Growth-and-income funds averaged a 292.5% gain over the past ten years in spite of the October 19th crash and several previous bear market cycles. Equity income funds performed even better gaining an average 325.8%. Funds are best suited for long term investment strategies that smooth out wildly fluctuating markets. Actually, a market crash creates buying opportunities. When fund shares decrease in value you can buy more shares.

The Vanguard Wellington balanced mutual fund realized a 316.1% gain over the past ten years for an average 15.4% annual yield. A 15% yield will double your money in five years. Higher risk growth funds can produce astronomical gains. The Fidelity Magellan growth Fund earned 1105.7% over the same time period.

Mutual funds offer professional money management, automatic dividend reinvestment, diversification, High yields, and relative safety of investment dollars. Funds are tailored to fit most investment goals from Money Market, Income, Tax Exempt, and Bond funds to Growth, Precious Metal, and Maximum Capital Gains.

Funds have minimum initial investments from zero to several thousand dollars and funds can automatically debit your checking or money market account monthly providing the discipline needed to build your account. When you purchase shares monthly, regardless of price fluctuations, your purchase price averages lower over time.

A funds total return is generated through dividend and capital gains distributions. Capital gains distributions are payments that reflect the increased value of the funds assets. If a fund buys 100 shares of company X at $10.00 per share and sells it for $20.00 the fund realizes a capital gain of $10.00 per share. Capital gains are distributed to fund investors along with dividend payments received from company X.

Of the over 2300 funds marketed approximately 300 are true no-load funds. A load is a sales commission paid to who ever is selling the fund. Commissions, loads, average from 2% to 8.5%. No-load funds only charge an annual advisors fee, typically less than 1%.

NO-LOAD MUTUAL FUNDS

Mutual funds are open-ended investments. Unlimited shares can be issued to satisfy all investor purchases. A no load mutual fund sells shares direct to the investor. If you invest $1000.00 in a no-load fund your entire $1000.00 purchases shares at the current market price. A 8.5% loaded fund would take $85.00 off the top leaving only $915.00 to purchase shares.

LOADS, COMMISSIONS & FEES

FRONT AND BACK END LOADS

A front end charge is used by most loaded funds. This charge is the difference between the buy and sell price. Back loads, redemption fees, are charged when the fund shares are sold. If a fund charges a 5% back load you will receive 5% less than the actual value when sold. Some funds have decreasing back loads. If you sell within the year purchased you would be charged a 5% back load. The load often decreases to zero after 5 years.

CONTINUOUS LOAD CHARGES

Mutual funds can be purchased through financial planners or stockbrokers. Certain funds have hidden loads to encourage financial planners to aggressively sell and market their product. A trailing fee is often charged of up to .75% of your total funds value annually. Another ploy is to reinvest your dividends at the offering price which can be up to 8.5% higher than the net asset value of the fund shares. If the full 8.5% was charged only 91.5% of your reinvested dividends would purchase new shares. You have essentially paid a front load on your reinvested dividends.

12b-1 CHARGES

Many funds charge up to 1.5% of your invested capital yearly for promotional and advertising expenses. A number of advertised no-load funds do charge 12-b1 expenses. The full amount of this charge is added to your taxable income even though you don't receive it. 12b-1 charges vary per fund. Look for a no-load fund that doesn't levy 12b-1 charges or charge low .25% or less maximum 12-b1 expenses. USA TODAY prints a "p" next to a funds listing indicating that 12-b1 fees are charged.

RECURRING FEES

All funds must pay expenses. Your

goal is to locate a no-load fund with low operating expenses. No-load funds average A 1.25% expense ratio. This pays fund operating costs and investment advisor's fee. Additionally 1% to 1.5% of your capital must be spent by the fund to buy and sell securities. See the statement of Additional Information in the prospectus for fee structure.

A comprehensive listing of no-load mutual funds is presented in the Individual Investor's Guide To No-Load Mutual Funds. This 368 page guide lists over 300 funds and provides a wealth of information on fund characteristics and selection. Including fee structures, expense ratios, minimum investments and performance ratings. The following excerpt is from their 1988 edition for the VANGUARD / WELLESLEY balanced no-load fund. Guidance is also included on how to read a funds prospectus, understanding mutual fund statements, recordkeeping, fund selection and much more. The guide sells for $19.95 and can be purchased direct from The American Association of Individual Investors, 612 North Michigan Avenue, Department NLG, Chicago, IL 60611.

Small opportunities
are often the beginnings
of great enterprises.

Demosthenes

VANGUARD/ WELLESLEY

Balanced

Vanguard Group
Vanguard Financial Center
Valley Forge, PA 19482
(800) 662-7447/(215) 648-6000

	Years Ending 12/31					
	1982	**1983**	**1984**	**1985**	**1986**	**1987**
Net Investment Income ($)	1.26	1.31	1.37	1.38	1.33	1.24
Dividends from Net Investment Income ($)	1.26	1.31	1.37	1.38	1.33	1.04
Net Gains (Losses) on Investments ($)	1.08	.84	.62	2.13	1.43	(1.52)
Distributions from Net Realized Capital Gains ($)	–	–	–	.10	.47	.38
Net Asset Value End of Year ($)	11.82	12.66	13.28	15.31	16.27	14.57
Ratio of Expenses to Net Assets (%)	.71	.70	.71	.60	.58	.49
Portfolio Turnover Rate (%)	60	38	36	21	31	40
Total Assets: End of Year (Millions $)	94.1	105.4	114.6	224.1	510.2	495.0
Annual Rate of Return (%) Years Ending 12/31	23.3	18.6	16.6	27.4	18.4	(1.9)

Five-Year Total Return(%)	Degree of Diversification	Beta	Bull (%)	Bear (%)
104.5[A]	NA	.29	78.5[C]	(4.0)[C]

Objective: Seeks to provide as much current income as management believes is consistent with reasonable risk. Invests approximately 70% of assets in investment grade fixed-income securities, with the balance invested in high yielding common stocks. May lend its portfolio securities and engage in repos.

Portfolio: (12/31/87) Corporate bonds 50%, common stocks 37%, U.S. government agency obligations 11%, repos 5%. Largest stock holdings: Union Electric Co., Pacific Gas & Electric Co.

Distributions: **Income:** Quarterly **Capital Gains:** Annually

12b-1: No

Minimum: **Initial:** $1,500 **Subsequent:** $100

Min IRA: **Initial:** $500 **Subsequent:** $100

Services: IRA, Keogh, Corp, 403(b), SEP, Withdraw, Deduct

Tel Exchange: Yes **With MMF:** Yes

Registered: All states

No-load funds are often identified in the newspapers financial section with an (NL) in the charge column next to a listed fund. If sell and buy columns are provided a NL will be printed in the buy column indicating that the funds buy and sell price are the same.

The sell column represents the price that the investor must pay to the fund to purchase one share. The buy column is the price the fund will pay to redeem shares from an investor. When the sell price is higher than the buy price the difference is the load or sales commission.

The performance of most loaded funds can be matched by a similar no-load fund. Loaded funds reduce your total return. You may find two funds with identical 5 year yields, one loaded and the other a no-load. The no-load fund would return more income because all of your initial investment would be earning dividends. Buying a loaded fund starts you off with a loss, the sales commission. Buy no-loads to put all of your money to work for you immediately.

INVESTMENT OBJECTIVES

The Investment Company Institute groups funds into 22 categories. Each financial publication uses its own classification system. MONEY Magazine groups its bond and stock funds into 18 categories. Diversity is a major benefit of mutual fund investing. There is a fund designed to satisfy even the most discriminating investor.

Aggressive Growth Funds

Maximum capital gains is sought through investments in small companies with low capitalization, out-of-favor stocks in depressed industries, new technologies or industries, and option trading. This is a highly speculative investment. Share prices fluctuate dramatically from bull to bear market. The Fidelity Magellan Fund was the stellar performer in this category over the past ten years with over 1100% growth recorded.

Balanced Funds

Invests to preserve your initial principal, seeks high dividend income, and looks for long-term principal and income growth. Portfolio of common stock, bonds, and preferred stock.

Corporate Bond Funds

Seeks income through investments in high yielding corporate bonds and often purchase a small portion in government bonds. Bond funds are interest sensitive. When interest rates increase bond prices decrease. If you purchased a bond paying 9% interest and the rates climbed to 10.5% your bonds would drop in value by 14%. However, if interest rates dropped to 6% you would realize a 42% capital gains on your investment.

Ginnie Mae Funds

Mortgages backed by the Government National Mortgage Association are purchased by these funds. Regulations prohibit fund diversity. Almost all of the funds assets must be invested in GNMA securities.

Global Bond Funds

Invests in bonds issued by foreign and domestic governments and companies.

Global Equity Funds

Invests in worldwide securities, including the United States. Specialty funds exist that purchase stock only in one or a related group of countries.

Growth Funds

Purchase common stock of companies that have growth potential and are financially sound. Capital gains are their primary objective to achieve significant share price appreciation. Dividend income is generally low and of little importance to growth fund financial planners.

Growth and Income Funds

Invests in companies that are experiencing average or above growth and pay sizable dividends. USA Today points out that stocks paying high dividends have consistently out performed other stock types and are a conservative investment. T. Rowe Price Associates indicate that Growth and Income stocks increased 292.5% over the past ten years. (EXCELLENT FOR CONSERVATIVE INVESTORS AND BEGINNER)

Equity Income Funds

The primary difference between growth and Income funds and equity income funds is the investment mix. Equity income funds invest a good portion, approximately 40%, of their funds assets in bonds. The remaining 60% is invested in high yielding quality stocks. (EXCELLENT FOR BEGINNERS AND CONSERVATIVE INVESTORS)

High Yield Bond Funds

Higher risk due to investing in lower grade bonds that historically pay higher dividends. The threat of bond default is greater with this type of investment.

Income Bond Fund

Invests in both government and corporate bonds to earn high current income.

International Funds

At least two-thirds of fund assets must be invested in overseas companies. Many specialized funds now exist that invest in just one country or a related group of countries.

Money Market Mutual Funds

Invests in the safest securities, including certificates of deposit, short term commercial paper, and Treasury bills. Generally invests only in short term securities. (The mutual fund with the least amount of risk). Yields are considerably less than growth and income or equity income funds. Price stability and preservation of principal is a primary objective. Very safe.

U.S. Government Income Funds

Invests in federally guaranteed mortgage-backed securities, Treasury bonds, and other government notes.

Precious Metals / Gold Funds

Two-thirds of the funds assets are invested in metal related securities. Also, substantial hard metal assets are owned in gold and silver bullion. (GENERALLY HELD FOR AN INFLATION HEDGE).

Only fifteen fund types are listed above. Their are also municipal bond funds, Long-Term and Short Term bond funds, Option Income Funds, etc. The funds listed above are a sampling of exactly how diverse the mutual fund market is. A fund for every appetite.

FUND DYNAMICS

Growth and income, equity income, balanced and total return funds have different names but similar objectives. These funds invest in bonds and high yield common stock providing greater share price stability than Growth Funds. These funds are lower risk conservative investments that seek a fair dividend return with possibilities for capital gains appreciation.

Fund share price is determined by adding the market values of all fund assets, stocks and bonds, and then dividing total market value by the number of shares outstanding. The share price is the NAV, Net Asset Value, and changes daily.

Funds build sizable selections of stocks, bonds, treasury notes and other investment vehicles to diversify and spread the risk.

Before buying into any fund you should call or write for a prospectus that explains investment goals and presents historical fund performance information for the past ten years. Toll free phone numbers are listed in Money Magazine's annual fund rating issue and in the Guide to Mutual Funds.

Over 2300 funds are listed alphabetically and by fund type in the new Guide to Mutual Funds. This 160 page guide also explains how funds operate, how to read a prospectus, how to purchase shares and much more. It is available for only $2.50, payable to the Investment Company Institute, to Guide to Mutual Funds, Investment Company Institute, 1600 M Street NW, Washington, DC 20036.

FUND SELECTION

Select a no-load fund that will meet your investment objectives and choose from the top performers over the long term, 10 years or more. A money market fund would provide safety with checkwriting privileges and earn favorable yields for those approaching retirement. Investors can assume greater risk for long term profits and invest in a growth fund. Growth fund share prices fluctuate dramatically from bull to bear markets. However, a young investor shouldn't be concerned about interim market swings. Long term investors benefit from bear markets by buying more shares as sales prices decrease.

Balanced funds are between the above two extremes. You assume some risk, yet are provided steady income through bonds and high yielding stock investments. The portfolio of stocks, bonds and other investment vehicles are balanced to offset each other during market cycles. This moderates the funds share price highs and lows during bear to bull market swings.

How much should you invest in a mutual fund? Mutual funds are ideal for accumulating wealth for future home purchases, retirement, and childrens education. An initial investment of

$250.00 with subsequent monthly $25.00 investments would appreciate to the amounts listed in table 5-1 after 10, 20 and 30 year periods at various interest rates.

TABLE 5-1

A $250 INITIAL INVESTMENT, INTEREST COMPOUNDED QUARTERLY, WITH $25.00 ADDED EACH MONTH WILL GROW TO THE FOLLOWING DOLLAR AMOUNTS IN 20 AND 30 YEAR PERIODS.

INTEREST	AMOUNTS IN ACCOUNT AFTER	
RATE	20 years	30 Years
8%	$15,726	$39,284
10%	$20,405	$59,886
12%	$26,735	$92,924
15%	$40,750	$184.491

For beginners a balanced fund, also called growth & income funds, is a good choice. When you become more knowledgeable about funds you can then investigate other alternatives. Many funds including the Vanguard and Value Line groups offer telephone switching. Telephone switching lets you transfer all or a portion of your balanced fund into a growth fund or any one of a dozen other fund types. If you feel the market is nearing its peak, you can switch to a money market or cash fund that provides share price stability and good yields in falling markets.

To begin your search call the Vanguard group toll free at 800-662-7447 and request their Vanguard Wellesly Balanced fund prospectus, minimum initial investment $1500.00. Obtain the Value Line Income Fund prospectus by calling 800-223-0818, minimum initial investment $1,000.00. The Loomis-Sayles Mutual fund at 800-345-4048 has a minimum initial investment of only $250.00 and had a 123.2% total return over the past five years. All three of these funds are true no-load balanced funds and do not charge 12b-1 expenses. There is no guaranty that funds you select will meet or exceed their previous growth rates. Money, Forbes, Consumer Reports and numerous other magazines rate funds annually. U.S.A. Today has many informative articles on mutual fund selection in their Money section.

Mutual funds offer professional management and financial growth for the small investor. Time invested in selecting and understanding funds can pay big dividends down the road. If you can spare $25.00 per month and a small initial investment you will be well on yourway to future financial security.

The secret to success is that
the harder you work
the luckier you get.

CHAPTER 6

DIVIDEND REINVESTMENT PLANS

You can buy stocks direct from over 1,000 corporations, pay low to no sales commission, often get a 5% discount on reinvested dividends, and buy as little as $10.00 dollars worth at a time in fractions of shares. Dividend reinvestment plans, DRP's, provide the beginning investor with a cost effective approach to stock accumulation.

T. Rowe Price Associates reported that approximately half of the total return experienced by the S & P 500 stocks has come from reinvested dividends over the past ten years. Reinvested dividends are critical to the growth of your investment. The ten highest paying dividend stocks of the 30 DJIA, Dow Jones industrial average, realized an annual total return of 18.4% from 1973 to 1988 according to John Slatter at Prescott Ball & Turben. Dividends attributed to 7.2% of the total return figure. During the same period the DJIA's total return for all 30 stocks was only 10.8%.

The above total return figures had to take sales commissions into consideration. Your total investment is reduced by stockbroker commissions. Yields would be higher if no sales commissions were paid. For example, a stock selling for $26 per share or $2,600 per 100 shares would cost an additional $40 to $100 in sales commissions. Discount brokers would charge the lower amount. AT & T currently sells for $26 per share. By investing $25.00 monthly in AT & T's DRP plan you would purchase .9615, slightly less than one, share of AT & T stock each month. All brokerage commissions are paid by AT & T. Each share earns $1.20 in dividends per year, 30 cents every three months. This amount is automatically reinvested to buy more shares. You also have the advantage of increased worth or capital gains if the stock increases in value. Over the past twelve months AT & T has sold for a low of $23 and a high of $33 per share. Companies retain your DRP shares in an account and send out quarterly statements. AT & T has a $5,000 maximum optional cash payment quarterly limit and no minimums. When you invest through a DRP plan you pay no stock brokers commissions, make additional purchases commission free, have dividends automatically reinvested and buy as little as a fraction of a share per month.

Mr. Robert Atkinson, financial analyst for Equitable Resources Corporation, an integrated energy company, related how Equitable stock has appreciated over the past 9 years. Robert said " Had you accumulated 100 shares of Equitable Resources in a DRP program in 1979 your investment would have been worth $3600. That same one hundred shares has grown through 4 stock splits to 675 shares with a current market value of $22,275. That's without considering reinvested dividends. Had you continued to contribute $25 per month plus reinvested your dividends your investment would have increased significantly." Equitable's DRP program began in 1972.

Many small investors discovered the advantages of Automatic Dividend Reinvestment Plans back in the 50's. The National Association Of Investors Corporation have seen many individuals start investment programs with as little as $10 or $20 a month, and build accounts worth over $100,000.

STOCK SELECTION

There are thousands of stocks to choose from. Your search will initially be limited to financially sound major corporations that pay a fare dividend plus have growth potential. Many of your selections will be from the S & P 500 index. Standard & Poor's corporation introduced this index back in 1957. The 500 companies are traded in the United

States stock markets and represent 80 industries comprising 68% of the total market value of stocks traded in the U.S..

Money, Money Maker, Better Investing, Fortune, Barons, and Business Week magazines along with U.S.A. Today, Investors Daily and the Wall Street Journal provide a wealth of information to the beginning investor. Money magazine is in my opinion the best for beginners. You will find numerous recommendations and stock tips in all of these publications. One issue of Money will provide numerous investment possibilities.

NAIC, National Association Of Investors Corporation, 1515 East Eleven Mile Road, Royal Oak, Michigan 48067 offers DRP investors a number of unique services. For an annual fee of $31.00 you receive an Investors Manual as well as a subscription to Better Investing magazine that features outstanding investment ideas each month. They present a 20 stock model portfolio and preview an undervalued stock in each issue. A comprehensive analysis is presented monthly for several companies. Numerous investor services are provided. They sponsor investment clubs, sell excellent training manuals, and teach fundamental stock analysis. You do not have to have any investment training to benefit from their programs.

It's not uncommon to favor several stocks or industries that you like or have a close association with. I have always liked Disney and Hershey foods. Disney's entertainment empire is growing leaps and bounds and their production studios have had numerous box office successes over the past 5 years. Remember Roger Rabbit! The food industry is recession resistant. You always have to eat no matter what the economy is up to. Check into your personal likes and dislikes for possible investments.

The quarterly statements from top performing balanced or growth and income funds reveal their top stock selections. These reports list all stocks and bonds owned by that fund. Generally, balanced funds are conservative and invest in high quality common stock that pay fair dividends and have potential for growth. You can follow their lead and research a few of their common stock picks.

Refer to chapter 9 for a mini DRP plan directory of stocks traded on the New York Stock Exchange. This list is not complete. For a comprehensive list with additional DRP characteristics for each company you can order one of the publication listed below or review a copy at your local library.

Standard & Poor's offers a $2 brochure listing close to 600 companies that have DRP programs. Write: Standard & Poor's Public Relations Dept, 25 Broadway, New York, N.Y. 10004. Evergreen Enterprises, P. O. Box 763, Laurel, Maryland 20707-0763, publishes a comprehensive Directory of companies offering dividend reinvestment plans. The directory lists 1,000 companies with details of each plan and costs $24.95. Over 700 of these companies offer no-cost purchase plans and some companies offer a 5 % discount off market price for reinvested dividends.

STOCK ANALYSIS

After identifying several interesting companies with DRP plans you must confirm that company's strengths and weaknesses before buying.

Mutual fund financial advisors select individual stocks and bonds for you. With a DRP you must select a stock to invest in. This is not as difficult as it seems. Especially when your focusing on Blue Chip, S & P 500 companies. There is an abundance of free services available at your local library. Several provide comprehensive stock rating systems that will help you make a selection.

Research all investments before buying. A company's strength and growth potential is not determined by weather or not they offer a DRP program. At your library review the Value Line Investment Survey Stock Analysis reports. Value Line publishes comprehensive detailed information sheets on 1,700 companies with historical data back 15 years. Five year highs and lows are projected and a detailed indepth company analysis is provided. Stocks are ranked 1 to 5 for safety and performance. Stick with a high 1 or 2 safety rating and a 1 to 3 rating for performance. Safety is your prime consideration. Company addresses are listed on each survey sheet. Note their address and send for DRP information.

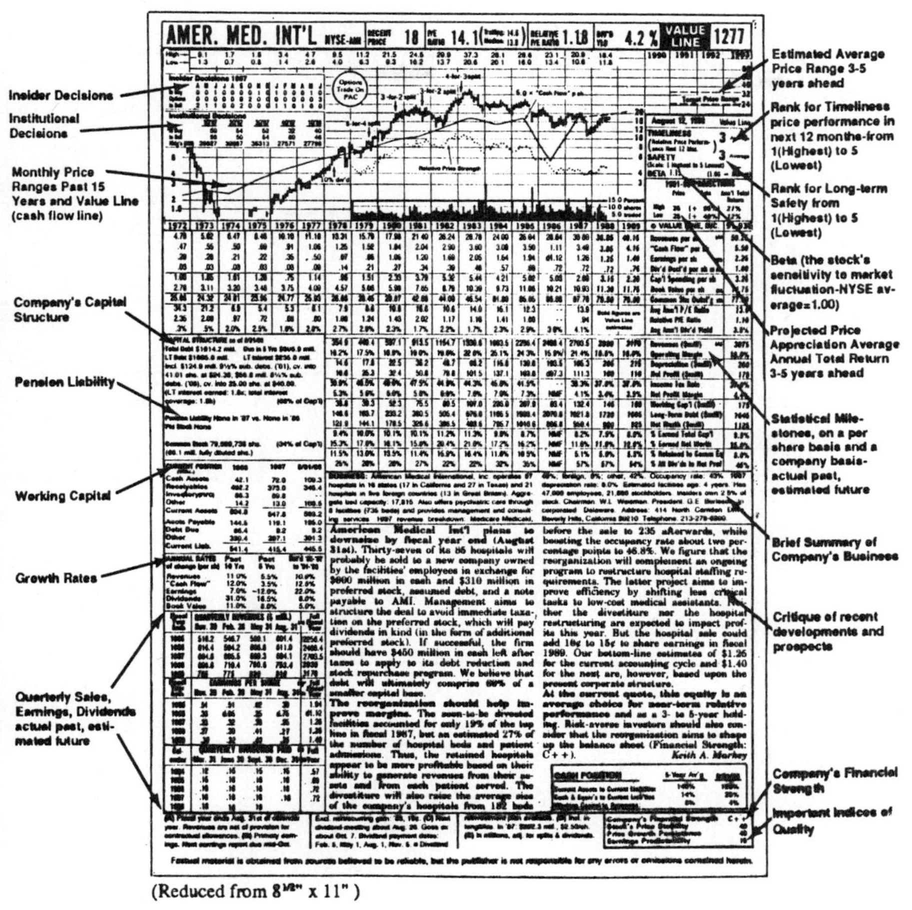

(Reduced from 8½" x 11")

The above Value Line Survey is reduced from it's normal 8 1/2" x 11" format. Note the sidebars explaining each section.

Standard and Poor's Corporate Records or Moody's Manuals list over 12,000 public companies with addresses, phone numbers and brief financial data. Standard & Poor's Stock Reports feature approximately 4300 stocks with financial analysis and a quality stock rating system. Value Line surveys are more comprehensive. They cover only the stronger companies and eliminate poor performers from their list quarterly. If you can't find a Value Line report then try Standard and Poor's or Moody's.

Focus on management when reading annual reports and survey sheets. Check to see how much stock the directors and upper management own. Generally, the greater percentage of ownership the more confidence you can have in the company.

NAIC teaches a fundamental approach to investing. They analyze a companies historical performance for the past ten years. A Stock Check List and an indepth 4 page Stock Selection Guide & Report is completed with the aid of a Value Line Survey or S & P report. Trend lines are drawn from the researched data and a determination is made concerning the companies strengths and weaknesses. Future high and low stock prices are projected and risk verses reward is analyzed.

NAIC markets a low cost computer stock evaluation program called Evaluform 3.0. This program operates with IBM, Apple Macintosh Plus, SE, II, Apple II and Apple Macintosh - 512. A 2.0 version is available for the commodore 64.

You can also rely on the many financial newsletters and services that present monthly stock recommendations.

PURCHASING STOCK

You must own at least one share of a company's stock to enroll in their Dividend Reinvestment Plan.

Your first share can be purchased from a stock broker, six companies, four of which are Fortune 500 companies, will sell their stock directly to investors or you can purchase stocks through the National Association of Investors Corporation.

NAIC can purchase stock for you in 42 companies with DRP programs such as Aetna Life & Casualty, Colgate-Palmolive Company, Walt Disney Corp, Gerber Products Company, McDonalds Corp, to name a few. NAIC is constantly adding companies to their selection list. Members send in a $5.00 transaction fee plus the cost of one share for the company they select. NAIC then purchases the stock for you. This is a considerable savings over purchasing your first share from a broker. Discount brokers typically charge a $35.00 minimum transaction fee.

When purchasing stock, have the certificates issued directly to you in your name. After purchasing your first shares you will be able to enroll in that companies DRP program. Companies generally send out enrollment information.

If you don't receive their DRP brochure within 4 to 6 weeks write for the information. After enrollment seven hundred companies that offer DRP's don't charge purchase fees. Therefore, for all future purchases, if you send $100.00 to purchase a stock selling for twenty dollars 5 full shares will be credited to your account. Had you purchased the same shares through a broker you could have purchased only 3 shares due to the $35.00 brokers transaction fee. 100% of your DRP invested money goes to work for you immediately.

Four fortune 500 companies that permit direct share purchase are:

Citicorp
Citicorp Individual Investor Relations
339 Park Avenue, 31st floor
New York, N.Y. 10043
Phone: 212-559-8263

W.R. Grace & Co.
1114 Avenue of the Americas
New York, N.Y. 10036
Phone: 800-472-2347

Great Northern Nekoosa Corp
P.O. Box 9309
Stamford, Conn 06904
Phone: 203-359-4000

Johnson Controls
C.O.: First Wisconsin Trust Co.
(Plan Administrator)
P.O. Box 2054
Milwaukee, Wis. 53201
Phone: 414-765-5806

Each of the above will permit investors to buy directly from the company. You do not need to purchase your first share from a stock broker or second party. Call or write for their DRP prospectus.

If you don't have the inclination or time to devote to research you may want to consider the companies listed below. These New York stock exchange companies yield over 6% and permit shareholders to reinvest dividends at a 5% discount. For each $100 of dividends earned you would receive $105 worth of stock when reinvested. Obtain the Value Line Survey sheets from your library. It will take you 15 minutes to copy these ten surveys. Bring them home, read them thoroughly, then decide. These ten selections were evaluated and recommended by Money Magazine in september 1988.

STOCK	Recent Price	PE	Yield
Chase Manhatten 212/552-7180	$29	NM	7.5%
Empire District Elec 417/623-4700	29	10	7.3
Green Mt. Power 802/864-5731	24	12	6.7
Hawaiian Electric 808/548-7302	28	12	6.7

Mortgage & Realty 215/782-2055	18	10	10.8
New Plan Reality 212/684-6200	14	19	6.3
NUI 201/685-3900	18	7	8.4
Santa Anita Realty 213/485-9220	31	19	6.5
S. Jersey Industries 609/561-9000	18	9	7.2
Texas Utilities 214/653-4646	28	6	10.1

Many companies offer long term growth potential and pay fair dividends. The following companies are all on the New York Exchange and worth researching.

American Telephone & Telegraph Company, A T & T. Current price $26, Dividend $1.20, Current Yield 4.6%. Call toll free at 800-348-8288.

2. Bell South, 5% discount on reinvested dividends, recent price $41, Dividend $2.20, Current Yield 5.4%. Call toll free at 800-631-6001.

3. Southwestern Bell Corp, c/o American Transtech, P.O. Box 45029, Jacksonville, FL 32232. Current Price 40, Dividend $2.48, Current Yield 6.2%. Call toll free at 800/351-7221.

4. Baltimore Gas and Electric Co., Charles Center, P.O. Box 1475, Baltimore, MD 21203. Current price $32.00, Dividend $2.00, Current Yield 6.2%. Phone 301/234-6501.

5. Northeast Utilities, P.O. Box 270, Hartford, CT 06141. Current price $20.75, Dividend $1.76, Current Yield 8.5%. Phone 203/244-5141.

Money Maker magazine rated the above stocks recession resistant in their February/March 1988 issue. I've been enrolled in AT & T and Bell South's DRP's for several years. These five companies can provide sizable total return over the next five years due to their excellent yield and potential for price appreciation.

ADVANTAGES OF DRP'S

DRP'S are long term investments. Market swings and daily price movements are of little concern. DRP's take most of the worry and fear out of investing as long as you invest in a solid company and review their performance regularly.

Most likely you will follow your investment in the daily paper. You shouldn't be upset when the price of your investment falls below your original purchase price. When prices fall you can purchase more shares. During the October 19th market decline AT & T fell from the mid thirties to just over twenty dollars per share. This didn't cause panic, it created an opportunity. That month I sent additional cash to purchase more shares through my DRP program. Falling prices create buying opportunities and as of February 26, 1988 AT & T has recovered to around $26.00.

Buying each month allows the small investor to DOLLAR COST AVERAGE. You buy more shares when the price is low and less when prices rise and your average cost per share decreases over time.

DRP's don't require additional monthly cash investments. Dividends earned will automatically be reinvested. It is up to you to send in additional monthly investment cash. PAY YOURSELF FIRST EACH PAYDAY. The first check I write is to one of my three DRP investments. Bi-weekly I rotate cash investments to my three DRP's. over a period of six weeks one payment has been sent to each. After writing my investment check for $25.00 I proceed to pay bills and set aside household money.

Remember, we restructured our finances to free up that $10 to $25 per month so it should be there for that purpose and that purpose only. Avoid the temptation to spend your recently discovered investment cash on personal items and your account will grow faster than you imagined.

Thomas OHara, Chairman of the Board of Trustees for NAIC, says " DRP's are a perfect way to apply the three principles that we find really helps an individual build a very sound and secure account. That is to invest reqularly over a long period of time, reinvest earnings and then try to put your money in companies that have prospects of being worth substantially more four or five years in the future. I believe the 40 or so companies we have in our program fit this category."

Many investors are attracted to the market when it is very active and moving upwards. Mr. OHara acknowledged that DRP investors do best in a down market and Better Investing magazine continually stresses this principle. I asked Mr. OHara for a factual account of an NAIC members financial growth and he related an incident that occurred at their annual meeting several years ago. He said " many individuals feel they have to buy into a high flying stock. We had a man get up at one of our meetings two years ago that insisted on telling his story in the middle of our luncheon. We let him tell his story and he said "he had been to an NAIC meeting 28 years ago and the idea of investing a little bit of money reqularly made some sense to him." He went back to his employer and asked them to take one days pay from his check each month and buy stock. His company, Toledo Edison, agreed to do that. Toledo Edison has been a good company but certainly not a high flyer of any kind. The gentleman said "you know, when I retired I was the biggest individual share holder in the company and my account was worth $1,300,000. I want everybody to know my retirement is just wonderful." Tom indicated that numerous NAIC regional meeting are scheduled throughout the country.

After accumulating 25 or so shares in one company consider diversification, buy into several sound companies in different market segments to spread risk.

Some companies purchase stock for their DRP investors each month and others quarterly. Check with your plan for specific purchase dates. There is a delay from the time you send in your payment to the actual purchase date. Plan participants have access to their account shares by calling or writing. If an emergency should arise you can cash in your investment.

DRP's offer an excellent opportunity for the small investor to build a sizable account, over time, for retirement, future purchases or unanticipated expenses. Many DRP's have no sales commissions, discounts on reinvested dividend purchases, and possibilities for appreciable long term capital gains.

CHAPTER 7

RETIREMENT PLANNING

Retirement planning requires long term savings and investment strategies that hedge against inflation and reduce current taxable income. The reduction in taxes provides additional investment cash. Over the past fifty years inflation has averaged just over 3 percent annually. Your investments must grow at or above the inflation rate to provide a comparable dollar per dollar value at retirement.

Most tax payers can take advantage of one or more legal tax shelters. Your home, U.S. Savings Bonds, and IRA's are some of the more common shelters available. A $1,000 yearly tax reduction, reinvested at 8% for thirty years, will grow to $113,280.

Tax shelters will help you keep more of your earnings by eliminating or deferring taxes. Many people simply don't bother with tax shelters. They consider them complex and mysterious. The majority of tax shelters, available to the average wage earner, are not difficult to implement or understand.

Before discussing available options take a look at where you are now financially. The October 1987 issue of Money magazine presented an excellent work sheet to calculate current and future assets. Major libraries should have a copy. Also, new subscribers to Money receive a pamphlet titled HOW TO Retire Worry Free. This pamphlet has a reprint of the October 1987 article "Figuring Your Future Fortune". The following chart will help you analyze your financial health.

FINANCIAL STATEMENT

ASSETS		LIABILITIES	
CASH:		CURRENT BILLS:	
Cash	.....	Credit Cards	.....
Checking Ac.	.....	Medical/Dental	.....
		Utility	.....
PERSONAL PROPERTY: (resale value)		Misc.	.....
		INSTALLMENT DEBT:	
Auto's	.....	Personal loans	.....
House	.....	Car payment	.....
Vacation home	.....	Charge accts	.....
Collectables	.....		
Jewelry	.....	TAXES OWED:	
Other	.....		
		Income Federal	.....
INVESTMENTS:		Income State	.....
		Property tax	.....
Savings ac.	.....	Local Wage tax	.....
CD's	.....		
Real estate	.....		
Bonds	.....	MORTGAGE DEBT:	
Stocks	.....		
Mutual Funds	.....	Home (1)	.....
Other	.....	Home (2)	.....
		Other	.....
PENSION PLANS:		TOTAL LIABILITIES	.....
IRA's	.....		
Company plan	.....	NET WORTH	
other	.....	Assets-Liabilities	
TOTAL ASSETS	$......		$......

After analyzing your personal net worth you will have a better feel for what needs to be done from an investors viewpoint. Your net worth is the difference between total assets less total outstanding liabilities. This is the amount you would have left after paying off all of your debts. Your net worth should steadily climb each year. You may be overloaded with debt and must restructure your debt as discussed in chapter one. Every dollar saved by lowering debt interest payments can go towards building a sound retirement nestegg. Don't be discouraged if your net worth hasn't grown over the past few years. Most new investors are in the same boat. Even with a heavy debt load, a savings and investment program should be started immediately. Remember, we're talking about $25.00 per month not hundreds of dollars each pay to get started.

One of the best ways to accumulate a retirement nestegg and reduce taxes is to invest in an IRA, Individual Retirement Account. The versatile IRA earns tax deferred income and for many tax payers contributions are deducted from taxable income.

IRA'S

Individual Retirement Accounts, are long term savings accounts that earn tax deferred interest and can also reduce your taxable income. IRA's are designed to supplement retirement income. Certain restrictions apply to deductible contributions and early withdrawals. A deductible contribution is the amount of your yearly IRA savings deposit that the IRS allows you to deduct from your income before calculating the taxes you owe.

Prior to investing in an IRA at least three times your monthly income should be saved in a conventional savings account, insured money market account or in short term certificates of deposit for emergencies. Secondly, you would want a separate savings for major purchases.

IRA's FOR THOSE NOT COVERED BY PENSIONS

You can deduct $2,000, the maximum yearly contribution, from taxable income no matter how much you earn. When a joint return is filed, and neither husband or wife have a retirement plan at work, $4000.00 can be contributed, placed into your IRA savings, and be deducted from your taxable income. If only one spouse works $2,250 can be deducted.

IRA's FOR THOSE COVERED BY A PENSION PLAN

A yearly contribution of $2,000 can be made to an IRA account, $4,000 if married and filing a joint return and $2250 if your spouse isn't employed. If total adjusted gross income isn't more than $25,000 for a single tax payer or $40,000 for a married couple filling jointly you can deduct the full maximum contribution.

Your deductible contribution decreases as your income increases above the limits specified in the preceding paragraph. You can still contribute the full $2,000 per worker, however the amount you can deduct from taxable income decreases $200 for each $1000 dollars over the lower limit as shown on the following chart.

LIMITS FOR IRA DEDUCTIONS PER PARTICIPANT IN WORK SPONSORED PENSION PLANS

LIMITS FOR IRA DEDUCTIONS
PER PARTICIPANT IN WORK-SPONSORED PENSION PLANS

Fileing status	Full $2,000 Deduction	Pro Rated Deduction	No Deduction
Joint	Up to $40,000	$40,000 to $50,000	Over $50,000
Single	Up to $25,000	$25,000 to $35,000	Over $35,000

Pro - rated deductions means that for each $1,000 of income you earn over the lower limits in the above chart, you lose $200 of deduction. If a single taxpayer, working for a company that has a pension plan, makes $28,000, they would lose $200 for each $1,000 earned over $25,000 or in this case $600 of deduction. He or she could still make the maximum contribution, however, only $1,400 could be taken off of taxable income before calculating the tax you would owe. The pro - rated feature also applies to a non working spouses contribution. A non working spouse is allowed to contribute $250 maximum. For each $1,000 over the lower limit earned on a joint return you must also deduct $25 of the non working spouses contribution.

TAX ADVANTAGES

Income earned on your IRA investments are tax deferred. If your IRA earned $500 interest and your income was $25,000 you would not add the $500 interest earned to your taxable income. Your tax would be calculated on $25,000 not $25,500. Secondly you are able to deduct the full $2,000 from your taxable income and will realize a substantial tax savings. For example, if you are single with an income of $25,000 your IRA contribution of $2,000 would reduce your taxable income to $23,000. Using 1987's tax tables you would pay $4,191 dollars tax for a single taxpayer on $23,000 taxable income. For $25,000 you would pay $4,751. By contributing $2,000 to an IRA you would save $560 in taxes. That's $560 more in your income tax return.

IRA's can be opened with banks, savings and loans, mutual funds , or with investment trusts. Banks offer long term 5, 10 and 15 year IRA Certificates of Deposit that traditionally offer higher interest than shorter term CD's. Self Directed IRA's can also be arranged with banks and brokerage houses. Self Directed IRA's permit the contributor to invest in common stock, art, collectibles, etc. Penalties are assessed for early withdrawal. Your IRA deposits should be money that you won't need until retirement. Otherwise, a 10% tax penalty is added for sums withdrawn prior to age 59 1/2. The penalty applies only if your contributions were deductible. If you were not able to deduct your contributions a penalty would only be assessed on the interest you earned on your IRA.

IRA's provide a method to accumulate a substantial amount towards retirement. Social Security may fall short when its our turn to collect. Higher interest is generally offered on IRA accounts and you don't have to contribute the full amount each year. Contribute only what you can afford. If you were able to save $2,000.00 per year in your IRA account, earning 8% compounded annually, you would have $344,640 after thirty five years. At age 59 1/2 you could take a lump sum payment or elect to receive a monthly allotment to supplement your retirement income. The amount withdrawn at retirement will be added to your income in the year withdrawn. Generally you will be in a lower tax bracket and pay less tax.

DISADVANTAGES

Your money will be tied up until age 59 1/2. Early withdrawal penalties are heavy. If you must withdraw your IRA cash you will be charged a 10% tax penalty for the amount withdrawn that was tax deductable or deferred.

OPENING AN IRA ACCOUNT

IRA'S are desirable if you would like to reduce your taxes and save for your retirement at the same time. Contact your local bank or credit union for details. Stock brokers and most mutual funds offer IRA accounts. If you know little about investing start with certificates of deposit or enter a growth and income mutual fund such as the Value line Income Fund, phone number 800-223-0818. Income funds are conservative investments that offer a fair return, possibilities of growth, and minimal risk. Do some research before you invest and you will be well on your way to future financial security. Many IRA accounts can be switched from one account type to another without penalty.

WORK SPONSORED RETIREMENT PLANS

401(k) plans:

Participation is strictly voluntary. A 401(k) plan reduces your taxable income. Up to 15% of your gross salary can be placed into a retirement account administered by a bank ,insurance company, etc.. Your contribution is not counted as income. If you gross $30,000 and your employer allows a 15% contribution you can contribute $4,500. This reduces your taxable income by $4,500 or in this example to $25,500. Each plan is structured differently. Your company may only permit a 5% or 10% contribution up to a limit of $7,313.

You can't withdraw your money until

age 59 1/2, change jobs, become disabled or suffer a financial hardship. Financial hardship must be proven and you must exhaust other financial resources first according to new IRS guidelines. If you do withdraw your funds early you are subject to a 10% early withdrawal penalty unless withdrawn for medical expenses that are over 7.5% of adjusted gross income.

401(k) plans permit larger contributions than IRA's and are one of the best ways to save for retirement. Taxable income is reduced and tax deferred income is earned until retirement. Many employers will match your contribution and some permit 401(k) loans. You can borrow a limited amount from your fund for up to five years at reasonable interest rates. The interest you pay goes back to your account. If you don't pay the loan back the outstanding loan principal will be subject to taxes and a 10 % penalty.

TAX-DEFERRED ANNUITIES

Tax-deferred annuities are sold through insurance companies and stockbrokers. They accrue tax deferred income until payments are received. An annuity is an agreement between two parties that provide payments, after a designated period of time, to the annuitant at specified monthly, quarterly or annual intervals. The contract can be paid for in one lump sum or installments. The company writing the plan offers an attractive interest rate for the desired term with a designated payment schedule. Annuities can be purchased in addition to other retirement plans. Unlike IRA's and

401(k) plans there is no tax deduction available for contributions. Withdrawal can begin at any specified interval without a tax penalty. These investment vehicles are ideal for college expenses and retirement.

When an annuity begins making payments the principal returned is not taxed. Taxes are paid only on the annuities tax deferred earned interest. Many companies offer a variety of unique annuity contracts. Some combine insurance packages, etc.

There are no-load annuities that do not charge a sales commission. These contracts often have a high early withdrawal penalty. Other loaded contracts charge up to an 8% commission. Read all of the fine print and don't hesitate to ask for advice if you don't understand the contract.

Defined benefit and defined contribution plans are the two types of pension plans offered by companies. The defined benefit plan pays a fixed annuity guaranteed by the company. The defined contribution plans, such as the 401(k), pays pension benefits based on the success of the investments in the plan. Benefits are not guarenteed. You can obtain a booklet titled " Protect Your Pension Money ", from the Pension Rights Center, 918 16th Street N.W., Suite 704, Washington DC 20006 for $6.

Social Security will be one of several income sources for your retirement. The Employee Benefit Research Institute predicts that for future retirees between the age of 32 and 41, 37.7% of their retirement income will come from Social Security, 36.6% from employer sponsored pensions, and 25.7% from savings and investments. If you earn $43,800 in 1988 you will collect $878 per month at age 65 from Social Security or approximately one forth of your salary. This doesn't account for inflation and future salary increases.

You can check your Social Security account by requesting form 7004, Request for Statement of Earnings, from your local SS office. Other retirement plans and investments future value can be estimated by using the charts from chapter one and two. Social Security may be a good part of our retirement however, a 75% reduction in income at age 65 would be hard to live with. Additional savings plans through one of the many options listed in this book will reduce the shock and increase our quality of retirement life significantly.

CHAPTER 8

REDUCE MORTGAGE COSTS

A home purchase is one of the biggest investments you can make. Total interest paid on a thirty year 9% mortgage is approximately twice the total loan principal. A thirty year $50,000 9% mortgage will cost $144,833 including principal and interest over the term of the loan. Interest payments and the loan term can be dramatically reduced by applying several little know techniques.

Debt reduction is a primary savings strategy. For example, you can save close to $400 in mortgage interest payments by adding $27.51 additional to your first payment on a 30 year 9%, $50,000 mortgage. That's quite a savings for $27.

A 30 year amortization schedule (30 year mortgage analysis chart) is included in this chapter. The $50,000 mortgage schedule lists all 361 payments extending from February 1989 to February 2019. The amount due is the total principal plus interest payment and does not change through out the 30 year term. Taxes are not included since they vary from community to community. The Principal column shows what dollar amount of your total monthly payment is applied to the principal. The first principal payment is only $27.31 and reduces your loan balance by that amount. Interest charged for the first month is $375. The total principal and interest columns provide total accumulated values for each category monthly.

There are two common methods used to dramatically reduce mortgage interest payments and reduce the term, years paid, at the same time. By using an amortization schedule tailored to your specific mortgage you can easily reduce a 30 year mortgage to 15 years and save thousands in interest payments.

METHOD ONE

This method requires increasing monthly mortgage payments by the principal amount due on the next payment. Refer to the amortization schedule in the back of this chapter. By paying the second payment's scheduled $27.51 principal payment with the first mortgage payment due on 2/89 a savings of $374.80 in interest is realized. The total principal paid on the loan is now $54.82. The second payment will be scheduled payment # 3 and an additional prepayment of $27.93, the principal due on payment #4, will be made.

Each even numbered principal payment paid in advance will reduce the mortgage term by one month and save the associated interest. In the first 2 1/2 years of the loan over $11,000 in interest payments will be saved, the mortgage term reduces by 2 1/2 years and the next payment will be #61 on the schedule. This is accomplished by paying an average additional monthly payment of only $33.64. With this method a mortgage payment is sent in each month with the next months principal included.

Not all mortgages permit prepayments. Check your mortgage for a no pre-payment penalty clause. Some institutions require minimum prepayments of from $50 to $250 monthly. Pay the specified minimum amount on your first payment. Add the additional principal amount to the total principal and start from that point on the amortization schedule for the next payment. You can then save for several months to accumulate another principal prepayment.

Principal payments increase over the length of the mortgage while interest payments decrease. The increasing prepayments are often offset by higher income levels resulting from annual salary increases.

AMORTIZATION SCHEDULES

Many financial institutions will sell you a mortgage amortization schedule for approximately $45. YOU CAN ORDER AMORTIZATION SCHEDULES DIRECT FROM D-Amp Publications for $30 plus $1.00 shipping and handling. Pennsylvania residents add $1.80 sales tax. Send the following data with payment to D-Amp Publications, 401 Amherst Avenue, Coraopolis, Pa. 15108.

1)Mortgage amount (Amount Financed)
2)Annual interest rate
3)Date first payment was due
4)Term of mortgage in years

METHOD TWO

A second accelerated payment plan allows borrowers to reduce mortgage term and interest paid out by half within the first three years of their mortgage. This plan requires 5 months additional principal payments each month for three years. Refer to the 30 year amortization schedule in this chapter. Your first payment would be $402.31 plus the principal due for payments 2,3,4,5, and 6 or a total additional payment of $138.61. The next monthly payment would include principal due for payments number 7 through 12 or $146.06 additional.

This system requires a much larger monthly additional payment. However, after three years payments fall back to only $402.31 for the remaining 12 years of the mortgage. You put out much more up front but have a much smaller payment for the remainder of the term. In the second year of the mortgage you would be paying $300 additional per month. This is more than most can afford.

These prepayment plans arn't as effective for Adjustable rate mortgages. The fluctuating rate requires a revised amortization schedule with each yearly rate adjustment. However, you will still reduce interest payments and mortgage term by the amount of principal prepayment.

Your total monthly mortgage payment will also include local property taxes and home owners insurance payments.

30 YEAR AMORTIZATION SCHEDULE
$50,000 AT A 9% ANNUAL RATE

Mortgage Calculator

Principal	Annual Rate	Term
$ 50000.00	9.00%	30/ 0

Payment Number	Date Due	Amount Due	Principal Due	Interest Due	Total Principal	Total Interest
1	2/89	402.31	27.31	375.00	0.00	0.00
2	3/89	402.31	27.51	374.80	27.31	375.00
3	4/89	402.31	27.72	374.59	54.82	749.80
4	5/89	402.31	27.93	374.38	82.54	1124.39
5	6/89	402.31	28.14	374.17	110.47	1498.77
6	7/89	402.31	28.35	373.96	138.61	1872.94
7	8/89	402.31	28.56	373.75	166.96	2246.90
8	9/89	402.31	28.78	373.53	195.52	2620.65
9	10/89	402.31	28.99	373.32	224.30	2994.18
10	11/89	402.31	29.21	373.10	253.29	3367.50
11	12/89	402.31	29.43	372.88	282.50	3740.60
12	1/90	402.31	29.65	372.66	311.93	4113.48
13	2/90	402.31	29.87	372.44	341.58	4486.14
14	3/90	402.31	30.10	372.21	371.45	4858.58
15	4/90	402.31	30.32	371.99	401.55	5230.79
16	5/90	402.31	30.55	371.76	431.87	5602.78
17	6/90	402.31	30.78	371.53	462.42	5974.54
18	7/90	402.31	31.01	371.30	493.20	6346.07
19	8/90	402.31	31.24	371.07	524.21	6717.37
20	9/90	402.31	31.48	370.83	555.45	7088.44
21	10/90	402.31	31.71	370.60	586.93	7459.27
22	11/90	402.31	31.95	370.36	618.64	7829.87
23	12/90	402.31	32.19	370.12	650.59	8200.23
24	1/91	402.31	32.43	369.88	682.78	8570.35
25	2/91	402.31	32.67	369.64	715.21	8940.23
26	3/91	402.31	32.92	369.39	747.88	9309.87
27	4/91	402.31	33.17	369.14	780.80	9679.26
28	5/91	402.31	33.41	368.90	813.97	10048.40
29	6/91	402.31	33.67	368.64	847.38	10417.30
30	7/91	402.31	33.92	368.39	881.05	10785.94
31	8/91	402.31	34.17	368.14	914.97	11154.33
32	9/91	402.31	34.43	367.88	949.14	11522.47
33	10/91	402.31	34.69	367.62	983.57	11890.35
34	11/91	402.31	34.95	367.36	1018.26	12257.97
35	12/91	402.31	35.21	367.10	1053.21	12625.33
36	1/92	402.31	35.47	366.84	1088.42	12992.43
37	2/92	402.31	35.74	366.57	1123.89	13359.27
38	3/92	402.31	36.01	366.30	1159.63	13725.84
39	4/92	402.31	36.28	366.03	1195.64	14092.14
40	5/92	402.31	36.55	365.76	1231.92	14458.17
41	6/92	402.31	36.82	365.49	1268.47	14823.93
42	7/92	402.31	37.10	365.21	1305.29	15189.42
43	8/92	402.31	37.38	364.93	1342.39	15554.63
44	9/92	402.31	37.66	364.65	1379.77	15919.56
45	10/92	402.31	37.94	364.37	1417.43	16284.21
46	11/92	402.31	38.23	364.08	1455.37	16648.58
47	12/92	402.31	38.51	363.80	1493.60	17012.66
48	1/93	402.31	38.80	363.51	1532.11	17376.46
49	2/93	402.31	39.09	363.22	1570.91	17739.97
50	3/93	402.31	39.38	362.93	1610.00	18103.19
51	4/93	402.31	39.68	362.63	1649.38	18466.12

Payment Number	Date Due	Amount Due	Principal Due	Interest Due	Total Principal	Total Interest
52	5/93	402.31	39.98	362.33	1689.06	18828.75
53	6/93	402.31	40.28	362.03	1729.04	19191.08
54	7/93	402.31	40.58	361.73	1769.32	19553.11
55	8/93	402.31	40.88	361.43	1809.90	19914.84
56	9/93	402.31	41.19	361.12	1850.78	20276.27
57	10/93	402.31	41.50	360.81	1891.97	20637.39
58	11/93	402.31	41.81	360.50	1933.47	20998.20
59	12/93	402.31	42.12	360.19	1975.28	21358.70
60	1/94	402.31	42.44	359.87	2017.40	21718.89
61	2/94	402.31	42.76	359.55	2059.84	22078.76
62	3/94	402.31	43.08	359.23	2102.60	22438.31
63	4/94	402.31	43.40	358.91	2145.68	22797.54
64	5/94	402.31	43.73	358.58	2189.08	23156.45
65	6/94	402.31	44.06	358.25	2232.81	23515.03
66	7/94	402.31	44.39	357.92	2276.87	23873.28
67	8/94	402.31	44.72	357.59	2321.26	24231.20
68	9/94	402.31	45.05	357.26	2365.98	24588.79
69	10/94	402.31	45.39	356.92	2411.03	24946.05
70	11/94	402.31	45.73	356.58	2456.42	25302.97
71	12/94	402.31	46.08	356.23	2502.15	25659.55
72	1/95	402.31	46.42	355.89	2548.23	26015.78
73	2/95	402.31	46.77	355.54	2594.65	26371.67
74	3/95	402.31	47.12	355.19	2641.42	26727.21
75	4/95	402.31	47.47	354.84	2688.54	27082.40
76	5/95	402.31	47.83	354.48	2736.01	27437.24
77	6/95	402.31	48.19	354.12	2783.84	27791.72
78	7/95	402.31	48.55	353.76	2832.03	28145.84
79	8/95	402.31	48.91	353.40	2880.58	28499.60
80	9/95	402.31	49.28	353.03	2929.49	28853.00
81	10/95	402.31	49.65	352.66	2978.77	29206.03
82	11/95	402.31	50.02	352.29	3028.42	29558.69
83	12/95	402.31	50.40	351.91	3078.44	29910.98
84	1/96	402.31	50.78	351.53	3128.84	30262.89
85	2/96	402.31	51.16	351.15	3179.62	30614.42
86	3/96	402.31	51.54	350.77	3230.78	30965.57
87	4/96	402.31	51.93	350.38	3282.32	31316.34
88	5/96	402.31	52.32	349.99	3334.25	31666.72
89	6/96	402.31	52.71	349.60	3386.57	32016.71
90	7/96	402.31	53.10	349.21	3439.28	32366.31
91	8/96	402.31	53.50	348.81	3492.38	32715.52
92	9/96	402.31	53.90	348.41	3545.88	33064.33
93	10/96	402.31	54.31	348.00	3599.78	33412.74
94	11/96	402.31	54.72	347.59	3654.09	33760.74
95	12/96	402.31	55.13	347.18	3708.81	34108.33
96	1/97	402.31	55.54	346.77	3763.94	34455.51
97	2/97	402.31	55.96	346.35	3819.48	34802.28
98	3/97	402.31	56.38	345.93	3875.44	35148.63
99	4/97	402.31	56.80	345.51	3931.82	35494.56
100	5/97	402.31	57.22	345.09	3988.62	35840.07
101	6/97	402.31	57.65	344.66	4045.84	36185.16
102	7/97	402.31	58.09	344.22	4103.49	36529.82

Mortgage Calculator

Principal	Annual Rate	Term
$ 50000.00	9.00%	30/ 0

Payment Number	Date Due	Amount Due	Principal Due	Interest Due	Total Principal	Total Interest
103	8/97	402.31	58.52	343.79	4161.58	36874.04
104	9/97	402.31	58.96	343.35	4220.10	37217.83
105	10/97	402.31	59.40	342.91	4279.06	37561.18
106	11/97	402.31	59.85	342.46	4338.46	37904.09
107	12/97	402.31	60.30	342.01	4398.31	38246.55
108	1/98	402.31	60.75	341.56	4458.61	38588.56
109	2/98	402.31	61.21	341.10	4519.36	38930.12
110	3/98	402.31	61.66	340.65	4580.57	39271.22
111	4/98	402.31	62.13	340.18	4642.23	39611.87
112	5/98	402.31	62.59	339.72	4704.36	39952.05
113	6/98	402.31	63.06	339.25	4766.95	40291.77
114	7/98	402.31	63.54	338.77	4830.01	40631.02
115	8/98	402.31	64.01	338.30	4893.55	40969.79
116	9/98	402.31	64.49	337.82	4957.56	41308.09
117	10/98	402.31	64.98	337.33	5022.05	41645.91
118	11/98	402.31	65.46	336.85	5087.03	41983.24
119	12/98	402.31	65.95	336.36	5152.49	42320.09
120	1/99	402.31	66.45	335.86	5218.44	42656.45
121	2/99	402.31	66.95	335.36	5284.89	42992.31
122	3/99	402.31	67.45	334.86	5351.84	43327.67
123	4/99	402.31	67.95	334.36	5419.29	43662.53
124	5/99	402.31	68.46	333.85	5487.24	43996.89
125	6/99	402.31	68.98	333.33	5555.70	44330.74
126	7/99	402.31	69.50	332.81	5624.68	44664.07
127	8/99	402.31	70.02	332.29	5694.18	44996.88
128	9/99	402.31	70.54	331.77	5764.20	45329.17
129	10/99	402.31	71.07	331.24	5834.74	45660.94
130	11/99	402.31	71.60	330.71	5905.81	45992.18
131	12/99	402.31	72.14	330.17	5977.41	46322.89
132	1/ 0	402.31	72.68	329.63	6049.55	46653.06
133	2/ 0	402.31	73.23	329.08	6122.23	46982.69
134	3/ 0	402.31	73.78	328.53	6195.46	47311.77
135	4/ 0	402.31	74.33	327.98	6269.24	47640.30
136	5/ 0	402.31	74.89	327.42	6343.57	47968.28
137	6/ 0	402.31	75.45	326.86	6418.46	48295.70
138	7/ 0	402.31	76.01	326.30	6493.91	48622.56
139	8/ 0	402.31	76.58	325.73	6569.92	48948.86
140	9/ 0	402.31	77.16	325.15	6646.50	49274.59
141	10/ 0	402.31	77.74	324.57	6723.66	49599.74
142	11/ 0	402.31	78.32	323.99	6801.40	49924.31
143	12/ 0	402.31	78.91	323.40	6879.72	50248.30
144	1/ 1	402.31	79.50	322.81	6958.63	50571.70
145	2/ 1	402.31	80.10	322.21	7038.13	50894.51
146	3/ 1	402.31	80.70	321.61	7118.23	51216.72
147	4/ 1	402.31	81.30	321.01	7198.93	51538.33
148	5/ 1	402.31	81.91	320.40	7280.23	51859.34
149	6/ 1	402.31	82.53	319.78	7362.14	52179.74
150	7/ 1	402.31	83.15	319.16	7444.67	52499.52
151	8/ 1	402.31	83.77	318.54	7527.82	52818.68
152	9/ 1	402.31	84.40	317.91	7611.59	53137.22
153	10/ 1	402.31	85.03	317.28	7695.99	53455.13

Mortgage Calculator

Principal	Annual Rate	Term
$ 50000.00	9.00%	30/ 0

Payment Number	Date Due	Amount Due	Principal Due	Interest Due	Total Principal	Total Interest
154	11/ 1	402.31	85.67	316.64	7781.02	53772.41
155	12/ 1	402.31	86.31	316.00	7866.69	54089.05
156	1/ 2	402.31	86.96	315.35	7953.00	54405.05
157	2/ 2	402.31	87.61	314.70	8039.96	54720.40
158	3/ 2	402.31	88.27	314.04	8127.57	55035.10
159	4/ 2	402.31	88.93	313.38	8215.84	55349.14
160	5/ 2	402.31	89.60	312.71	8304.77	55662.52
161	6/ 2	402.31	90.27	312.04	8394.37	55975.23
162	7/ 2	402.31	90.94	311.37	8484.64	56287.27
163	8/ 2	402.31	91.63	310.68	8575.58	56598.64
164	9/ 2	402.31	92.31	310.00	8667.21	56909.32
165	10/ 2	402.31	93.01	309.30	8759.52	57219.32
166	11/ 2	402.31	93.70	308.61	8852.53	57528.62
167	12/ 2	402.31	94.41	307.90	8946.23	57837.23
168	1/ 3	402.31	95.11	307.20	9040.64	58145.13
169	2/ 3	402.31	95.83	306.48	9135.75	58452.33
170	3/ 3	402.31	96.55	305.76	9231.58	58758.81
171	4/ 3	402.31	97.27	305.04	9328.13	59064.57
172	5/ 3	402.31	98.00	304.31	9425.40	59369.61
173	6/ 3	402.31	98.74	303.57	9523.40	59673.92
174	7/ 3	402.31	99.48	302.83	9622.14	59977.49
175	8/ 3	402.31	100.22	302.09	9721.62	60280.32
176	9/ 3	402.31	100.97	301.34	9821.84	60582.41
177	10/ 3	402.31	101.73	300.58	9922.81	60883.75
178	11/ 3	402.31	102.49	299.82	10024.54	61184.33
179	12/ 3	402.31	103.26	299.05	10127.03	61484.15
180	1/ 4	402.31	104.04	298.27	10230.29	61783.20
181	2/ 4	402.31	104.82	297.49	10334.33	62081.47
182	3/ 4	402.31	105.60	296.71	10439.15	62378.96
183	4/ 4	402.31	106.40	295.91	10544.75	62675.67
184	5/ 4	402.31	107.19	295.12	10651.15	62971.58
185	6/ 4	402.31	108.00	294.31	10758.34	63266.70
186	7/ 4	402.31	108.81	293.50	10866.34	63561.01
187	8/ 4	402.31	109.62	292.69	10975.15	63854.51
188	9/ 4	402.31	110.45	291.86	11084.77	64147.20
189	10/ 4	402.31	111.27	291.04	11195.22	64439.06
190	11/ 4	402.31	112.11	290.20	11306.49	64730.10
191	12/ 4	402.31	112.95	289.36	11418.60	65020.30
192	1/ 5	402.31	113.80	288.51	11531.55	65309.66
193	2/ 5	402.31	114.65	287.66	11645.35	65598.17
194	3/ 5	402.31	115.51	286.80	11760.00	65885.83
195	4/ 5	402.31	116.38	285.93	11875.51	66172.63
196	5/ 5	402.31	117.25	285.06	11991.89	66458.56
197	6/ 5	402.31	118.13	284.18	12109.14	66743.62
198	7/ 5	402.31	119.01	283.30	12227.27	67027.80
199	8/ 5	402.31	119.91	282.40	12346.28	67311.10
200	9/ 5	402.31	120.81	281.50	12466.19	67593.50
201	10/ 5	402.31	121.71	280.60	12587.00	67875.00
202	11/ 5	402.31	122.63	279.68	12708.71	68155.60
203	12/ 5	402.31	123.55	278.76	12831.34	68435.28
204	1/ 6	402.31	124.47	277.84	12954.89	68714.04

Principal	Annual Rate	Term
$ 50000.00	9.00%	30/ 0

Payment Number	Date Due	Amount Due	Principal Due	Interest Due	Total Principal	Total Interest
205	2/ 6	402.31	125.41	276.90	13079.36	68991.88
206	3/ 6	402.31	126.35	275.96	13204.77	69268.78
207	4/ 6	402.31	127.29	275.02	13331.12	69544.74
208	5/ 6	402.31	128.25	274.06	13458.41	69819.76
209	6/ 6	402.31	129.21	273.10	13586.66	70093.82
210	7/ 6	402.31	130.18	272.13	13715.87	70366.92
211	8/ 6	402.31	131.16	271.15	13846.05	70639.05
212	9/ 6	402.31	132.14	270.17	13977.21	70910.20
213	10/ 6	402.31	133.13	269.18	14109.35	71180.37
214	11/ 6	402.31	134.13	268.18	14242.48	71449.55
215	12/ 6	402.31	135.13	267.18	14376.61	71717.73
216	1/ 7	402.31	136.15	266.16	14511.74	71984.91
217	2/ 7	402.31	137.17	265.14	14647.89	72251.07
218	3/ 7	402.31	138.20	264.11	14785.06	72516.21
219	4/ 7	402.31	139.23	263.08	14923.26	72780.32
220	5/ 7	402.31	140.28	262.03	15062.49	73043.40
221	6/ 7	402.31	141.33	260.98	15202.77	73305.43
222	7/ 7	402.31	142.39	259.92	15344.10	73566.41
223	8/ 7	402.31	143.46	258.85	15486.49	73826.33
224	9/ 7	402.31	144.53	257.78	15629.95	74085.18
225	10/ 7	402.31	145.62	256.69	15774.48	74342.96
226	11/ 7	402.31	146.71	255.60	15920.10	74599.65
227	12/ 7	402.31	147.81	254.50	16066.81	74855.25
228	1/ 8	402.31	148.92	253.39	16214.62	75109.75
229	2/ 8	402.31	150.04	252.27	16363.54	75363.14
230	3/ 8	402.31	151.16	251.15	16513.58	75615.41
231	4/ 8	402.31	152.30	250.01	16664.74	75866.56
232	5/ 8	402.31	153.44	248.87	16817.04	76116.57
233	6/ 8	402.31	154.59	247.72	16970.48	76365.44
234	7/ 8	402.31	155.75	246.56	17125.07	76613.16
235	8/ 8	402.31	156.92	245.39	17280.82	76859.72
236	9/ 8	402.31	158.09	244.22	17437.74	77105.11
237	10/ 8	402.31	159.28	243.03	17595.83	77349.33
238	11/ 8	402.31	160.47	241.84	17755.11	77592.36
239	12/ 8	402.31	161.68	240.63	17915.58	77834.20
240	1/ 9	402.31	162.89	239.42	18077.26	78074.83
241	2/ 9	402.31	164.11	238.20	18240.15	78314.25
242	3/ 9	402.31	165.34	236.97	18404.26	78552.45
243	4/ 9	402.31	166.58	235.73	18569.60	78789.42
244	5/ 9	402.31	167.83	234.48	18736.18	79025.15
245	6/ 9	402.31	169.09	233.22	18904.01	79259.63
246	7/ 9	402.31	170.36	231.95	19073.10	79492.85
247	8/ 9	402.31	171.64	230.67	19243.46	79724.80
248	9/ 9	402.31	172.92	229.39	19415.10	79955.47
249	10/ 9	402.31	174.22	228.09	19588.02	80184.86
250	11/ 9	402.31	175.53	226.78	19762.24	80412.95
251	12/ 9	402.31	176.84	225.47	19937.77	80639.73
252	1/10	402.31	178.17	224.14	20114.61	80865.20
253	2/10	402.31	179.51	222.80	20292.78	81089.34
254	3/10	402.31	180.85	221.46	20472.29	81312.14
255	4/10	402.31	182.21	220.10	20653.14	81533.60

Mortgage Calculator

Principal	Annual Rate	Term
$ 50000.00	9.00%	30/ 0

Payment Number	Date Due	Amount Due	Principal Due	Interest Due	Total Principal	Total Interest
256	5/10	402.31	183.58	218.73	20835.35	81753.70
257	6/10	402.31	184.95	217.36	21018.93	81972.43
258	7/10	402.31	186.34	215.97	21203.88	82189.79
259	8/10	402.31	187.74	214.57	21390.22	82405.76
260	9/10	402.31	189.14	213.17	21577.96	82620.33
261	10/10	402.31	190.56	211.75	21767.10	82833.50
262	11/10	402.31	191.99	210.32	21957.66	83045.25
263	12/10	402.31	193.43	208.88	22149.65	83255.57
264	1/11	402.31	194.88	207.43	22343.08	83464.45
265	2/11	402.31	196.34	205.97	22537.96	83671.88
266	3/11	402.31	197.82	204.49	22734.30	83877.85
267	4/11	402.31	199.30	203.01	22932.12	84082.34
268	5/11	402.31	200.80	201.51	23131.42	84285.35
269	6/11	402.31	202.30	200.01	23332.22	84486.86
270	7/11	402.31	203.82	198.49	23534.52	84686.87
271	8/11	402.31	205.35	196.96	23738.34	84885.36
272	9/11	402.31	206.89	195.42	23943.69	85082.32
273	10/11	402.31	208.44	193.87	24150.58	85277.74
274	11/11	402.31	210.00	192.31	24359.02	85471.61
275	12/11	402.31	211.58	190.73	24569.02	85663.92
276	1/12	402.31	213.16	189.15	24780.60	85854.65
277	2/12	402.31	214.76	187.55	24993.76	86043.80
278	3/12	402.31	216.37	185.94	25208.52	86231.35
279	4/12	402.31	218.00	184.31	25424.89	86417.29
280	5/12	402.31	219.63	182.68	25642.89	86601.60
281	6/12	402.31	221.28	181.03	25862.52	86784.28
282	7/12	402.31	222.94	179.37	26083.80	86965.31
283	8/12	402.31	224.61	177.70	26306.74	87144.68
284	9/12	402.31	226.30	176.01	26531.35	87322.38
285	10/12	402.31	227.99	174.32	26757.65	87498.39
286	11/12	402.31	229.70	172.61	26985.64	87672.71
287	12/12	402.31	231.43	170.88	27215.34	87845.32
288	1/13	402.31	233.16	169.15	27446.77	88016.20
289	2/13	402.31	234.91	167.40	27679.93	88185.35
290	3/13	402.31	236.67	165.64	27914.84	88352.75
291	4/13	402.31	238.45	163.86	28151.51	88518.39
292	5/13	402.31	240.23	162.08	28389.96	88682.25
293	6/13	402.31	242.04	160.27	28630.19	88844.33
294	7/13	402.31	243.85	158.46	28872.23	89004.60
295	8/13	402.31	245.68	156.63	29116.08	89163.06
296	9/13	402.31	247.52	154.79	29361.76	89319.69
297	10/13	402.31	249.38	152.93	29609.28	89474.48
298	11/13	402.31	251.25	151.06	29858.66	89627.41
299	12/13	402.31	253.13	149.18	30109.91	89778.47
300	1/14	402.31	255.03	147.28	30363.04	89927.65
301	2/14	402.31	256.95	145.36	30618.07	90074.93
302	3/14	402.31	258.87	143.44	30875.02	90220.29
303	4/14	402.31	260.81	141.50	31133.89	90363.73
304	5/14	402.31	262.77	139.54	31394.70	90505.23
305	6/14	402.31	264.74	137.57	31657.47	90644.77
306	7/14	402.31	266.73	135.58	31922.21	90782.34

Mortgage Calculator

Principal	Annual Rate	Term
$ 50000.00	9.00%	30/ 0

Payment Number	Date Due	Amount Due	Principal Due	Interest Due	Total Principal	Total Interest
307	8/14	402.31	268.73	133.58	32188.94	90917.92
308	9/14	402.31	270.74	131.57	32457.67	91051.50
309	10/14	402.31	272.77	129.54	32728.41	91183.07
310	11/14	402.31	274.82	127.49	33001.18	91312.61
311	12/14	402.31	276.88	125.43	33276.00	91440.10
312	1/15	402.31	278.96	123.35	33552.88	91565.53
313	2/15	402.31	281.05	121.26	33831.84	91688.88
314	3/15	402.31	283.16	119.15	34112.89	91810.14
315	4/15	402.31	285.28	117.03	34396.05	91929.29
316	5/15	402.31	287.42	114.89	34681.33	92046.32
317	6/15	402.31	289.58	112.73	34968.75	92161.21
318	7/15	402.31	291.75	110.56	35258.33	92273.94
319	8/15	402.31	293.94	108.37	35550.08	92384.50
320	9/15	402.31	296.14	106.17	35844.02	92492.87
321	10/15	402.31	298.36	103.95	36140.16	92599.04
322	11/15	402.31	300.60	101.71	36438.52	92702.99
323	12/15	402.31	302.85	99.46	36739.12	92804.70
324	1/16	402.31	305.12	97.19	37041.97	92904.16
325	2/16	402.31	307.41	94.90	37347.09	93001.35
326	3/16	402.31	309.72	92.59	37654.50	93096.25
327	4/16	402.31	312.04	90.27	37964.22	93188.84
328	5/16	402.31	314.38	87.93	38276.26	93279.11
329	6/16	402.31	316.74	85.57	38590.64	93367.04
330	7/16	402.31	319.12	83.19	38907.38	93452.61
331	8/16	402.31	321.51	80.80	39226.50	93535.80
332	9/16	402.31	323.92	78.39	39548.01	93616.60
333	10/16	402.31	326.35	75.96	39871.93	93694.99
334	11/16	402.31	328.80	73.51	40198.28	93770.95
335	12/16	402.31	331.26	71.05	40527.08	93844.46
336	1/17	402.31	333.75	68.56	40858.34	93915.51
337	2/17	402.31	336.25	66.06	41192.09	93984.07
338	3/17	402.31	338.77	63.54	41528.34	94050.13
339	4/17	402.31	341.31	61.00	41867.11	94113.67
340	5/17	402.31	343.87	58.44	42208.42	94174.67
341	6/17	402.31	346.45	55.86	42552.29	94233.11
342	7/17	402.31	349.05	53.26	42898.74	94288.97
343	8/17	402.31	351.67	50.64	43247.79	94342.23
344	9/17	402.31	354.31	48.00	43599.46	94392.87
345	10/17	402.31	356.96	45.35	43953.77	94440.87
346	11/17	402.31	359.64	42.67	44310.73	94486.22
347	12/17	402.31	362.34	39.97	44670.37	94528.89
348	1/18	402.31	365.06	37.25	45032.71	94568.86
349	2/18	402.31	367.79	34.52	45397.77	94606.11
350	3/18	402.31	370.55	31.76	45765.56	94640.63
351	4/18	402.31	373.33	28.98	46136.11	94672.39
352	5/18	402.31	376.13	26.18	46509.44	94701.37
353	6/18	402.31	378.95	23.36	46885.57	94727.55
354	7/18	402.31	381.79	20.52	47264.52	94750.91
355	8/18	402.31	384.66	17.65	47646.31	94771.43
356	9/18	402.31	387.54	14.77	48030.97	94789.08
357	10/18	402.31	390.45	11.86	48418.51	94803.85

Principal	Annual Rate	Term
$ 50000.00	9.00%	30/ 0

Payment Number	Date Due	Amount Due	Principal Due	Interest Due	Total Principal	Total Interest
358	11/18	402.31	393.38	8.93	48808.96	94815.71
359	12/18	402.31	396.33	5.98	49202.34	94824.64
360	1/19	404.34	401.33	3.01	49598.67	94830.62
361	2/19	0.00	0.00	0.00	50000.00	94833.63

MONTHLY PAYMENTS TO BANK
TO AMORTIZE EACH $1000 OF LOAN

loan Term	Percent Interest 10%	10.5%	11%	11.5%	12%
10 Yrs	13.21	13.49	13.76	14.06	14.35
15 Yrs	10.75	11.05	11.37	11.69	12.01
20 Yrs	9.65	9.99	10.33	10.67	11.02
25 Yrs	9.09	9.44	9.81	10.17	10.54
30 Yrs	8.78	9.15	9.53	9.91	10.29

The above chart can be used to determine the total monthly interest plus principal payment for loans made between 10% and 12% interest rates. If $50,000 was borrowed at 11% for thirty years you would look down the 11% column until you come to the 30 Yrs row. Use the factor of 9.53 to multiply times the amount of the loan in thousands of dollars. (50 x 9.53 = $476.50) Your interest plus principal payment would be $476.50. Taxes plus insurance premiums would be added to this figure to arrive at your total monthly mortgage payment.

CHAPTER 9

DIVIDEND REINVESTMENT PLAN

DIRECTORY

The following directory is a partial list of companies on the New York Stock Exchange that offer Dividend Reinvestment Plans. Numerous plans are administered by second parties. Plan administrators can operate more than one plan. The company name and phone number is listed. Call for current plan information. If you would prefer to write obtain company addresses from the S & P or Value Line Survey sheets found at major libraries. A comprehensive DRP directory is marketed by Evergreen Enterprises, Laurel, MD 20707-0763 for $19.95. Their directory lists over 1000 companies on all exchanges. Company addresses and specific plan information is provided for each listing. Many companies on the American and OTC exchanges also offer DRP's.

Research each stock as explained in chapter 6 before making any purchases.

AAR Corp	312/439-3939
Abbott Laboratories	617/929-6320
ACME Electric Corp	716/373-3050
ACME Clevelan Corp	216/687-5742
Adams Express Co	301/752-5900
ADT INC	212/558-1100
Advest Group Inc.	203/525-1421
Aetna Life & Casualty Co	203/273-3977
Air Products & Chemicals	215/481-8760
Alcan Aluminum LTD	514/848-8050
Alco Standard Corp	215/296-8000
Allegheny International	412/562-5051
Allegheny Power Systems	212/752-2121
Allen Group Inc	516/293-5500
Allied-Signal Inc	201/455-2127
Allis-Chalmers Corp	414/475-3670
Alltel Corp	216/650-7000

Aluminum Co Of America	412/553-4706
Amax Inc	800-243-4000
Amerada Hess Corp	212/997-8500
American Brands Inc	203/698-5000
American Business Products Inc	404/434-1000
American Can Co.	203/552-2829
American Cyanamid Co	212/530-8052
American Electric Power	800/237-2667
American Express Co	212/640-5694
American Family Corp	404/323-3431
American General Corp	800/392-4136
American Heritage Life Investment corp	904/359-2539
American Home Products Corp	212/868-5000
American Standard Inc	212/703-5100
American Telephone & Telegraph	800/348-8288
Ameritech	800/233-1342
Ames Department Stores	203/563-8234
AMFEC INC	415/772-3300
AMOCO Corp	312/856-6111

AMP Inc	717/564-0100
Amsouth Bankcorp	205/326-5794
Anchor Hocking Corp	614/687-2127
Anheuser-Busch Cos	314/577-2039
Apache Corp	612/347-8700
Arizona Public Service Co	800/457-2983
ARKLA Inc	800/527-7844
ARMCO INC	513/425-2516
ARMSTRONG WORLD INDUSTRIES INC	717/396-2810
ASA LIMITED	201/635-0122
ASARCO INC	212/510-2000
ASHLAND OIL INC	606/329-3333
ATLANTIC CITY ELECTRIC CO	609/645-4100
ATLANTIC RICHFIELD CO	213/486-3611
AVERY INTERNATIONAL	818/304-2000
AVNET INC	212/644-1050
AVON PRODUCTS INC	212/546-6015
AZP GROUP INC	800/457-2983
BAKER INTERNATIONAL CORP	714/634-2333

BALL CORP	317/747-6472
BALTIMORE GAS AND ELECTRIC CO	301/234-6501
BANC ONE CORP	614/463-5944
BANK OF BOSTON	617/434-2200
BANK OF NEW YORK CON INC	212/530-1784
BANKAMERICA CORP	415/622-3456
BANKERS TRUST NEW YORK	800/221-4096
BARD (CR) INC	201/277-8000
BARNES CROUP INC	203/583-7070
BARRY WRIGHT CORP	212/613-7147
BOUSCH AND LOMB INC	716/338-6045
BAY STATE GAS CO	617/828-8650
BECTON, DICKINSON $ Co	212/587-6515
BELL AND HOWELL CO	312/470-7100
BELL ATLANTIC CORP	800/631-2355
BELLSOUTH CORP	800/631-6001
BEMIS CO INC	612/340-6000
BENEFICIAL CORP	302/798-0800
BETHLEHAM STEEL CORP	212/587-6515
BEVERLY ENTERPRISES	818/577-6111
BLACK AND DECKER CORP	301/583-3900

BLACK HILLS CORP	605/348-1700
BLOCK (H & R) INC	816/753-6900
BOISE CASCADE CORP	208/384-7590
BORDEN INC	212/573-4000
BORG-WARNER CORP	312/322-8500
BOSTON EDISON CO	617/424-2667
BRIGGS AND STRATTON CORP	414/259-5496
BRISTOL-MYERS CO	212/546-4347
BROOKLYN UNION GAS CO	800/221-6891
BRUNSWICK CORP	312/470-4291
BURLINGTON INDUSTRIES INC	919/379-2909
BRUNDY CORP	203/852-8440
CABOT CORP	717/825-1173
CALIFORNIA REAL ESTATE INVESTMENT TRUST	415/433-1805
CAMPBELL SOUP CO	609/342-3585
CAPITAL HKHHOLDING CORP	502/560-2000
CARLISLE COS INC	513/241-2500
CAROLINA FREIGHT CORP	704/435-6811
CAROLINA POWER 6 LIGHT CO	800/334-4374

CARPENTER TECHNOLOGY GROUP	212/587-6515
CASCADE NATURAL GAS CORP	206/624-3900
CASTLE & COOKE INC	415/986-3000
CATERPILLAR INC	309/675-1000
CBI INDUSTRIES INC	312/654-7366
CBS INC	212/975-4321
CELANESE CORP	212/719-8000
CENTEL CORP	312/399-2500
CENERIOR ENERGY CORP	800/362-3206
CENTRAL AND SOUTH SOUTH WEST CORP	800/527-5797
CENTRAL HUDSON GAS	914/486-5204
CENTRAL ILLINOIS PUBLIC SERVICE CO	217/525-5521
CENTRAL LOUISIANA ELECTRIC CO INC	318/484-7400
CENTRAL MAINE POWER CO	207/623-3521
CENTRAL VERMONT PUBLIC SERVICE CORP	804/773-2711
CENTURY TELEPHONE ENTERLPRISES INC	318/387-5541
CHAMPION INTERNATIONAL	203/358-7000
CHAMPION PRODUCTS INC	716/385-3200
CHAMPION SPARK PLUG CO	419/535-2567

CHASE MANHATTAN CORP	212/552-7180
CHEMED CORP	513/762-6988
CHEMICAL NEW YORK CORP	212/608-8429
CHEVRON	415/894-7700
CHRYSLER CORP	313/956-2076
CHUBB CORP	201/580-2000
CIGNA CORP	215/241-4979
CINCINNATI BELL INC	800/354-0400
CINCINNATI GAS & ELECTRIC	513/632-3655
CINCINNATI MILICRON INC	800/354-0400
CITICORP	800/223-9201
CLARK EQUIPMENT CO	219/239-0100
CLOROX CO	415/271-1561
CNA INCOME SHARES INC	312/822-4181
COCA COLA CO	404/676-2777
COLGATE-PALMOLIVE CO	212/587-6515
COLT INDUSTRIES INC	212/940-0501
COLUMBIA GAS SYSTEM	302/429-5725
COMMONWEALTH EDISON CO	800/253-1122
COMMONWEALTH ENERGY SYSTEM	800/447-1183
CONNECTICUT ENERGY COR	203/368-6781

CONNECTICUT NATURAL GAS CORP	203/727-3203
CONRAC CORP	203/348-2100
CONSOLIDATED NATURAL GAS	312/227-1000
CONTEL CORP	404/391-8027
CONTINENTAL CORP	212/618-7147
CONTROL DATA CORP	612/853-6701
COOPER INDUSTRIES INC	713/739-5400
COPPEERWELD CORP	412/263-3200
CORNING GLASS WORKS	716/258-5833
CP NATIONAL CORP	415/397-8580
CPC INTERNATIONAL INC	201/894-2460
CUMMINS ENGINE CO INC	312/407-4880
CYCLOPS	412/343-4000

DANS CORP	800/537-8823
DAYTON HUDSON CORP	612/370-6948
DEAN FOODS CO	312/461-2121
DEERE & CO	309/752-8000
DELMARVA POWER 6 LIGHT CO	302/429-3355
DELTA AIR LINES INC	404/765-2443

DENNISON MANUFACTURING CO	212/587-6515
DETROIT EDISON CO	313/237-8666
DEXTER CORP	203/244-5141
DI GIORGIO CORP	415/765-0100
DISNEY (WALT) PRODUCTIONS	818/505-7001
DIVERSIFIED EMERGIES INC	612/342-5101
DOMMINION RESOURCES INC	800/368-7012
DOW CHEMICAL CO	517/636-1463
DOW JONES & CO INC	212/416-2601
DRAVO COPR	412/566-3000
DRESSER INDUSTRIES	214/740-6708
DU PONT DE NEMOURS & CO	302/774-0910
DUKE POWER CO	800/438-0142
DUQUESNE LIGHT CO	800/247-0400
E-SYSTEMS INC	214/698-5698
EASTERN UTILITIES ASSOCIATES	617/357-9590
EASTMAN KODAK CO	716/724-4000
EATON CORP	216/523-5000
EMERSON ELECTRIC	314/553-2000
EMHART CORP	203/244-5141

EMPIRE DISTRICT ELECTRIC	417/623-4700
ENGELHARD CORP	201/632-6000
ENSEARCH CORP	800/ENSERCH
ENSEARCH EXPLORATION PARTNERS LTD	800/ENSEARCH
EQUIFAX INC	404/885-8000
EQUIMARK CORP	412/288-5359
EQUITABLE RESOURCES CO	412/553-5877
EXCELSIOR INCOME SHARES	212/425-7120
EXXON CORP	212/333-6900
FAIRCHILD INDUSTRIES INC	703/478-5800
FAY'S DRUG CO INC	315/451-8000
FEDERAL NATIONAL MORTGAGE ASSN	212/613-7147
FEDERAL PAPER BOARD CO INC	201/391-1776
FEDERAL SIGNAL CORP	617/929-6563
FEDERAL DEPARTMENT STORES	212/613-7147
FERRO CORP	216/641-8580
FIRESTONE TIRE & RUBBER CO	212/613-7059
FIRST BANK SYSTEMS INC	612/370-5100
FIRST CHICAGO CORP	312/732-6980

FIRST FIDELITY BANCORP	201/430-4917
FIRST FINANCIAL FUND INC	212/214-1215
FIRST INTERSTATE BANCORP	818/992-7138
FIRST MISSISSIPPI CORP	601/948-7550
FIRST VIRGINIA BANKS INC	703/241-3669
FIRST WISCONSIN CORP	414/765-4321
FLEET FINANCIAL GROUP INC	401/278-6242
FLEMING COS INC	405/840-7200
FLORIDA PROGRESS CORP	813/895-1736
FORD MOTOR CO	313/222-4381
FORT HOWARD PAPER CO	414/435-8821
FOSTER WHEELER CORP	212/530-8055
FOX PHOTO INC	713/236-4646
FRANCE FUND INC	212/906-7733
GAF CORP	201/628-3000
GANNETT CO INC	703/284-6000
GATX CORP	312/621-6599
GENCORP	216/798-3000
GENERAL CINEMA CORP	617/232-8200
GENERAL ELECTRIC CO	203/373-2816

GENERAL MILLS INC	612/540-2311
GENERAL MOTORS CORP	313/556-5000
GENERAL NUTRITION INC	412/288-4725
GENERAL SIGNAL CORP	203/357-8800
GEROGIA-PACIFIC CORP	404/521-5210
GERBER PRODUCTS CO	404/521-4000
GILLETTE CO	617/421-7000
GLEASON CORP	716/473-1000
GOODRICH CO	216/374-3985
GOODYEAR TIRE & RUBBER CO	216/796-1617
GORDON JEWELRY CORP	713/222-8080
GOULD INC	312/640-4181
GRACE (W R) & CO	800/GRACE-IR
GREAT NORTHERN NEKOOSA CORP	203/359-4000
GREAT WEATERN FINANCIAL CORP	213/852-3411
GREEN MOUNTAIN POWER CO	802/864-5731
GROW GROUP INC	212/599-4400
GRUMMAN CORP	212/530-8444
GTE CORP	203/965-2000
GULF+WESTERN INDUSTRIES	212/333-3700

GULF STATES UTILITIES CO	800/231-9266
HANDLEMAN CO	313/362-4400
HANDY & HARMAN	212/207-2690
HARRIS CORP	305/727-9283
HARSCO CORP	201/440-5900
HAWAIIAN ELECT INDUST INC	704/548-7302
HEILEMAN BREWING CO INC	201/440-5900
HEINZ CO (HJ)	412/456-5700
HERCULES INC	212/613-7147
HERSHEY FOODS CORP	717/534-7526
HEXCEL CORP	415/956-3333
HOLLY SUGAR CORP	201/440-5900
HOMESTAKE MINING CO	415/981-8150
HONEYWELL INC	612/870-6887
HORIZON BANCORP	201/539-7700
HOSPITAL CORP OF AMERICA	615/327-9551
HOUGHTON MIFFLLIN CO	617/929-6575
HOUSTON INDUSTRIES INC	713/229-7588
HUFFY CORP	513/449-8792
HUGHES TOOL CO	713/222-0686

IC INDUSTRIES	312/565-3169
IDAHO POWER CO	800/635-5406
IE INDUSTRIES	319/398-4644
ILLINOIS POWER CO	217/424-6609
INDIANA ENERGY INC	317/927-0610
INGERSOLL-RAND CO	212/530-8065
INLAND STEEL INDUSTRIES	312/346-0300
INTER-CITY GAS CORP	204/944-9920
INTERNATIONAL BUSINESS MACHINES CORP	212/735-7000
INTERNATIONAL MULTIFOODS	612/340-3300
INTERNATIONAL PAPER CO	212/613-7147
INTERSTATE POWER CO	319/582-5421
IOWA PUBLIC SERVICE CO	800/538-1382
IOWA RESOURCES INC	800/247-5211
IOWA-ILLINOIS GAS & ELECT	319/326-7326
IPALCO ENTERPRISES INC	317/261-8394
ITALY FUND INC	617/328-5000
ITT CORP	212/940-2990

JIM WALTER CORP	813/871-4467
JOHNSON & JOHNSON	201/524-0400
JOHNSON CONTROLS INC	414/765-5806
JORGENSEN CO	213/567-1122
JOSTEN'S INC	612/830-3300
JOY MANUFACTURING CO	412/562-4500
KAISER ALUMINUM & CHEMICAL CORP	212/587-6515
KANNNNSAS CITY POWER AND LIGHT	816/556-2053
KANSAS GAS & ELECTRIC CO	316/261-6640
KANSAS POWER & LIGHT CO	913/296-1950
KELLOGG CO	616/961-2765
KENNAMETAL INC	412/539-5204
KENTUCKY UTILITIES CO	606/255-1461
KERR-McGEE CORP	405/231-6711
KIDDE INC	212/608-8440
KIMBERLY-CLARK CORP	414/721-2421
KNIGHT-RIDDER INC	305/350-2650
KRAFT INC	212/613-7147
KROGER CO	513/762-4969

LAFARGE CORP	214/991-6800
LEAR SIEGLER INC	213/452-8869
LEASEWAY TRANSPORTATION	216/464-3300
LEHMAN CORP	800/221-5350
LILLY CO	800/833-8699
LIMITED INC	212/613-7147
LONE STAR INDUSTRIES	201/440-5900
LOUISIANA-PACIFIC CORP	503/221-0800
LOUISVILLE GAS & ELECT CO	502/566-4011
LOWE'S COS INC	919/651-4000
LUCKY STORES INC	415/833-6000
MACMILLIAN INC	212/613-7147
MANHATTAN INDUSTRIES INC	212/221-3700
MANHATTAN NATIONAL CORP	212/484-9519
MANUFACTURERS HANOVER CORP	212/613-7147
MARINE MIDLAND BANKS INC	718/843-2424
MARION LABORATORIES INC	816/966-4000
MARTIN MARIETTA CORP	301/897-6309
MAYTAG CO	515/792-7000

MCA INC	201/440-5900
MEAD CORP	513/222-6323
MELLON BANK CORP	412/391-5210
MERCK & CO INC	201/574-6883
MERRILL LYNCH & CO	212/637-7466
MICHIGAN CONSOL GAS CO	703/790-7641
MICHIGAN ENERGY RESOURCES	313/242-4100
MIDDLE SOUTH UTILITIES	504/569-4360
MIDWEST ENERGY CO	712/277-7400
MINNESOOTA MINING & MFG CO	612/291-5194
MINNESOTA POWER & LIGHT	218/723-3936
MOBIL CORP	201/440-5900
MONSANTO CO	314/694-1000
MONTANA POWER CO	800/245-6767
MORGAN (JP) & CO	212/483-3166
MOTOROLA INC	312/397-5000
McDONALDS CORP	312/887-3395
McGRAW HILL INC	212/512-2000
McKESSON CORP	415/983-8300

NATIONAL FUEL GAS CO	212/613-7147
NATIONAL GYPSUM CO	212/587-6515
NATIONAL MINE SERVICE CO	412/281-0688
NATIONAL-STANDARD CO	616/683-8100
NBD BANCORP INC	313/225-1000
NCR CORP	216/697-5745
NEVADA POWER CO	702/367-5613
NEW ENGLAND ELECT SYS	617/366-9011
NEW YORK STATE ELECTRIC ABD GAS CORP	800/225-5NGE
NEWMONT MINING CORP	212/953-6900
NIAGARA MOHAWK POWER CO	800/448-5450
NICOR INC	312/242-4470
NORFOLK SOUTHERN CORP	703/981-4592
NORSTAR BANCORP INC	518/447-4043
NORTHEAST UTILITIES	203/244-5141
NORTHERN STATES POWER CO	800/329-8226
NORTHROP CORP	212/613-7147
NORTON CO	617/795-2199
NORWEST CORP	612/338-5718

NUCOR CORP	704/366-7000
NYNEX CORP	800/358-1133
OAKITE PRODUCTS INC	201/464-6900
OCCIDENTAL PETROLEUM CORP	213/879-1700
OHIO EDISON CO	800/633-4766
OKLAHOMA GAS & ELECT CO	405/272-3213
OLIN CORP	212/613-7052
ONEIDA LTD	315/361-3391
OUTBOARD MARINE CORP	312/689-6200
OWENS CORNING FIBERGLAS	419/248-8000
OWENS ILLINOIS INC	419/247-2928
PACIFIC GAS & ELECT CO	415/972-2033
PACIFIC LIGHTING CORP	213/689-3481
PACIFIC TELESIS GROUP	800/637-6373
PACIFICORP	800/233-5453
PAINE WEBBER GROUP INC	212/713-2722
PENNEY (J C) CO INC	212/957-4321
PENNSYLVANIA POWER & LIGHT	800/345-3085
PENNZOIL CO	713/546-4000

PEOPLES ENERGY CORP	312/431-4292
PEPSICO INC	914/253-2000
PERKIN-ELMER CORP	203/762-1000
PFIZER INC	212/573-3704
PHELPS DODGE CORP	212/613-7198
PHILADELPHIA ELECT CO	800/223-7326
PHILIP MORRIS COS INC	212/880-5000
PHILLIPS PETROLEUM CO	212/613-7147
PIEDMONT NATURAL GAS CO	800/438-8410
PILLSBURY CO	612/330-5449
PITNEY BOWES INC	203/356-7165
POLAROID CORP	617/577-2000
PORTLAND GENERAL CO	503/225-6474
POTOMAC ELECTRIC POWER CO	202/872-2797
PPG INDUSTRIES INC	412/434-2120
PRIMARK CORP	703/790-7641
PROCTER & GAMBLE CO	513/562-1100
PUBLIC SERVICE CO OF COLORADO	303/571-7663
PUBLIC SERVICE CO OF NEW MEXICO	800/545-4425
PUGET SOUND POWER & LIGHT	206/462-3719

PUROLATOR COURIER INC	201/953-6400
QUAKER OATS CO	800/621-9525
QUAKER STATE OIL REFINING CORP	814/676-7676
QUESTAR CORP	801/534-5886
RALSTON PURINA CO	314/982-1000
RANCO INC	614/764-3733
RAYTHEON CO	617/862-6600
READING & BATES	918/583-8521
REPUBLICBANK CORP	214/922-4297
REXHAM CORP	704/541-2800
REYNOLDS METALS CO	804/281-4764
RITE AID CORP	717/761-2633
RJR NABISCO INC	919/773-2356
ROBERTSON (HH) CO	412/281-3200
ROCHESTER GAS & ELECTRIC CORP	716/546-2700
ROCHESTER TELEPHONE CORP	716/323-7579
ROCKWELL INTERNATIONAL	412/565-2000
ROLLINS INC	404/888-2000

ROPER GROUP INC	215/628-6541
RYDER SYSTEMS INC	305/593-3726
ST JOSEPH LIGHT & POWER	816/233-8888
SALOMON INC	212/764-3700
SAN DIEGO GAS & ELECT CO	619/696-2020
SARA LEE CORP	312/726-2600
SAVANNAH ELECTRIC & POWER CO	912/232-7171
SCANA CORP	803/748-3656
SCHERING-PLOUGH CORP	201/822-7000
SCOTT PAPER CO	215/522-5000
SEALED POWER CORP	616-724-5011
SEARS ROEBUCK & CO	212/406-5458
SECURITY PACIFIC CORP	818/507-2215
SHAKLEE CORP	415/954-3000
SHERWIN WILLIAMS CO	216/687-5745
SIERRA PACIFIC RESOURCES	800/662-7575
SIGNET BANKING CORP	804/771-7793
SMITH INTERNATIONAL	714/752-9000
SMITHKLINE BECKMAN CORP	215/751-5128
SMUCKER (JM) CO	216/682-0015

SOUTHEAST BANKING CORP	305/577-3000
SOUTHERN CO	404/393-4498
SOUTHERN INDIANA GAS & ELECTRIC CO	812/464-4553
SOUTHERN UNION	214/748-8511
SOUTHLAND CORP	800/527-7844
SOUTHERN GAS CORP	702/876-9800
SOUTHWESTERN BELL CORP	800/351-7221
SOUTHWESTERN ENERGY CO	501/521-1141
SQUARE D CO	312/397-2600
SQUIBB CORP	609/921-4000
STANDARD OIL CO	216/586-5229
STANLEY WORKS	203/225-5111
STERLING DRUG CO	212/907-2000
STEVENS (JP) & CO	212/930-2000
SREWART-WARNER CORP	312/883-6000
STRIDE RITE CORP	617/491-8800
SUN CO INC	215/977-3922
SUN ELECTRIC CORP	815/459-7700
SUN TRUST BANKS INC	404/588-7817

TAFT BROADCASTING CO	800/354-0400
TALLEY INDUSTRIES	212/613-7147
TEMPLE-INLAND INC	409/829-1313
TENNECO INC	713/757-3907
TEXACO INC	914/253-6072
TEXAS EASTERN CORP	800/231-7543
TEXAS UTILITIES CO	214/653-4646
TEXTRON INC	212/587-6396
THOMAS & BETTS CORP	201/685-1600
TIDEWATER INC	212/613-7147
TIME INC	212/522-1212
TIMKEN CO	216/438-3376
TNP ENTERPRISES CO	817/731-0099
TORO CO	612/887-8526
TRACTOR INC	800/527-7844
TRANSAMERICA CORP	212/613-7147
TRAVELERS CORP	203/277-5986
TRIANGLE INDUSTRIES INC	212/230-3000
TRINOVA	419/247-4856
TRW INC	800/442-2001
TWIN DISC INC	414/634-1981

U S WEST INC	800/537-0222
UGI CORP	215/337-1000
UNION CAMP CORP	201/628-2000
UNION CARBIDE CORP	914/789-3657
UNION ELECTRIC	314/554-3502
UNION PACIFIC CORP	212/418-7800
UNITED JERSEY BANKS	609/987-3200
UNITED STATES SHOE CORP	513/527-7000
UNITED STATES TOBACCO CO	513/527-7000
UNITED TELECOMMUNICATIONS	913/676-3345
UNIVERSAL FOODS CORP	414/271-6755
UNIVERSAL LEAF TOBACCO CO INC	804/359-9311
UNOCAL CORP	213/977-7817
UPJOHN CO	616/323-5258
USF&G CORP	301/547-3000
USG CORP	312/321-4294
USX CORP	412/433-4803
UTAH POWER & LIGHT	801/535-4131
VARIAN ADSSOCIATES INC	415/493-4000

VESTAUR SECURITIES INC	215/786-7202
VF CORP	215/378-1151
VULCAN MATERIALS	205/877-3204
WALGREEN CO	312/940-2936
WARNER COMMUNICATIONS INC	212/484-8000
WARNER-LAMBERT CO	201/540-2728
WASHINGTON GAS & LIGHT CO	202/624-6410
WASHINGTON NATIONAL CORP	312/570-3208
WASHINGTON WATER POWER CO	509/589-0500
WASTE MANAGEMENT INC	312/654-8800
WEIS MARKETS INC	717/286-4571
WELLS FARGO & CO	212/613-7147
WENDY'S INTERNATIONAL INC	212/587-6515
WESTERN UNION CORP	212/613-7147
WESTVACO CORP	212/688-5000
WEYERHAEUSER CO	206/924-2345
WHIRLPOOL CORP	616/926-5000
WHITTAKER CORP	212/613-7147
WICOR INC	414/291-7000
WINN-DIXIE STORES	904/783-5000

WISCONSIN ELECTRIC POWER	414/277-2786
WISCONSIN GAS CO	414/291-7000
WISCONSIN POWER & LIGHT	800/356-5343
WITCO CORP	212/605-3800
WOOLWORTH CO	212/553-2000
WRIGLEY JR CO	312/644-2122
WYLE LABORATORIES	800/221-2856
XEROX CORP	800/828-6396
ZENITH ELECTRONICS CORP	312/391-7000
ZERO CORP	213/846-4191
ZURN INDUSTRIES INC	216/687-5745

CHAPTER TEN

Tracking Your Investments

Certain data must be recorded to track investment performance and for tax purposes. Refer to the stock record sheet on page 137. Before placing stock certificates in your safety deposit box list: purchase date, certificate number, company name, number of shares, price per share, total purchase price, brokerage commission, and tax basis per share. When selling stock you will need to record the sales date, number of shares sold, total sales price and the gain or (loss) of the transaction.

Every stock has an assigned unique number with a letter prefix. List this number on the stock record form. If a certificate is lost it can be replaced by notifying the company of the certificate number, the number of shares stated on the certificate, your tax ID number or social security #, and your individual account number if applicable.

The tax basis per share will be the stock price plus commission. If 100 shares are purchased at $20 per shares and a commission of $75 is charged the tax basis includes the commission. In this example your basis would be $2,075 divided by 100 shares or $20.75 per share.

When you sell your shares another $75 commission will be charged by your broker. If you sell 100 shares at $30 per share you would receive $3,000 less $75 commission or $2,925. This figure would be placed in the Total Sales Price column. To determine loss or gain you would subtract the total purchase price of $2,075 from the total sales price of $2,925 and list a gain of $850.

Tax basis per share is calculated to determine gain or loss when less shares are sold than originally purchased. It isn't uncommon to purchase 200 shares of a company's stock and after a significant price increase take a profit by selling off one half or 100 shares. You could still retain 100 shares for long term appreciation.

STOCK RECORD

Purchase Date	Certificate Number	Co. Name	Number Of Shares	Price Per Share	Total Purchase Price	Brokerage Commission	Tax Basis Per Share	Sale Date	# Shares Sold	Total Sales Price	Gains or Loss

A second form , refer to page 39, will help you keep track of your dividend reinvestment stock purchase plans and mutual funds. You would use one Security Record for each investment plan or security. NAIC uses a similar form that can be ordered in an 8 1/2" by 11" format. The following Security Record can tell you in an instant what your total investment is. By dividing the "Total Cost All" figure by "Total Shares Owned" you will arrive at your average cost per share. This is where you will see the benefits of DOLLAR COST AVERAGING . You can also calculate total yearly and accumulated dividends and total gain or loss by multiplying your total shares owned by the current market value and comparing it to your total cost column. The data for these forms are taken directly from statements received from mutual funds or dividend reinvestment plans. You should retain your yearly statements for as long as you own the security. The statements will be your proof of purchase and will establish profit or loss when taxes are filed.

In addition to the above records you must keep stock sale and purchase brokerage receipts, called confirmation of transaction slips, for up to six years after the security is sold. This also applys to mutual fund yearly summary statements and your DRP account statement. If the IRS hasn't initiated an audit of your return within six years after filed you can discard the copies.

DIVIDEND RECORD

COMPANY NAME ____________________

Dividend pay date	# of Shares	Paid per Share	Total Rec'd This Pay-ment	Total Rec'd Year To Date	Grand Total

SECURITY RECORD

COMPANY NAME ____________________

Date Pur-chased	No of Shares Bought	Total Shares Owned	Cost Per Share	Total Cost This Buy	Total Cost All

List all financial data in a central location. The following information is helpful to have on file for two reasons. First is will help organize and manage your finances. Secondly, you and others, if need be, can use this organizer to handle your affairs.

LIFE INSURANCE DATA

Name of agent: ____________________
Phone #: ____________________

Policy location: ____________________

1st Policy #: ____________ Amount: ______
Company: ____________________
2nd Policy #: ____________ Amount: ______
Company: ____________________
3rd Policy #: ____________ Amount: ______
Company: ____________________

Group policy insurance

1st Policy #: ____________ Amount: ______
Company: ____________________
2nd Policy #: ____________ Amount: ______
Company: ____________________

AUTO INSURANCE

Location of policies: ____________________
Agent: ______________ Phone #: __________
Company: ____________________

Policy #: ____________________
Policy #: ____________________
Policy #: ____________________

FINANCIAL DATA

Stocks owned:
Certificate location:

1. ____________________ # of shares: __________
2. ____________________ " __________
3. ____________________ " __________
4. ____________________ " __________
5. ____________________ " __________
6. ____________________ " __________
7. ____________________ " __________
8. ____________________ " __________
9. ____________________ " __________

List Mutual Funds owned:
File location:

1. ____________________ # of shares: __________
2. ____________________ " __________
3. ____________________ " __________
4. ____________________ " __________

Cerificates of Deposit:
Location: ______________________________

1. certificate number: ________ Amount: ____
2. certificate number: ________ " : ____
3. certificate number: ________ " : ____

Other securities owned:
Location: ______________________________

1. ______________________________
2. ______________________________
3. ______________________________
4. ______________________________

Name of stock broker: ____________________
Phone number: ______________

Location of tax records and canceled checks: ______________________________

Credit Cards:

Name	No.	Exp Date
1. ______________________________		______
2. ______________	____________	______
3. ______________	____________	______
4. ______________	____________	______
5. ______________	____________	______
6. ______________	____________	______
7. ______________	____________	______

BANKING DATA

Bank names	acc. #	phone #
1. ____________	__________	____________
2. ____________	__________	____________
3. ____________	__________	____________
4. ____________	__________	____________

Safe deposit box location: ______________
Box number: _________

Location of box key: ____________________

Location of will: ______________________
____

Executor: ______________________________

Location of important papers: ___________
____

Attorney's name: _______________________
____

EMPLOYMENT DATA

Employer's name: _______________________

Address;: ______________________________
____
____

Phone number: _______________

Immediate Supervisor: __________________

Social Sec #: ____________________

REAL ESTATE DATA

Description of residence and lenders name:
____
____
____

Rental property description and lenders name: _________________________________
____
____
____

Location of mortgages, deeds, etc.:

File the above information where your spouse or next of kin can locate it if needed. You may also wish to note your medical insurer and specific plan data and group numbers. This information is not complete. Add other specific data that pertains to your needs. Once you get your records in order spend the time to keep them current. It takes only a few minutes to update or change data on this list. If you are lucky enough to have a computer data file system updating will be that much easier.

> If we spent half as much time learning how to take risks as we spend avoiding them, we wouldn't have nearly so much to fear in life.
>
> Dr. E. Paul Torrance

CHAPTER 11

Investment Term Glossary

Accrued interest: Interest earned on a bond or certificate of deposit since the last payout was received. CD's interest generally accrues throughout the term and is paid out when the certificate is redeemed.

Amortization: Debt reduction with level payments equal to the interest and principal owed through the debts's term. See chapter 8 for a $50,000, 30 year, 9% amortization schedule.

Annuity: An agreement between two parties that provide payments, after a period of time, to the annuitant at specified monthly, quarterly, or annual intervals.

Appreciation: Increased value of your investment. A companies worth above it's book value.

Assets: A item of value listed in an annual report. Generally income producing.

At-the market: A buy or sell order to a stock broker at the current market price of the security.

Balance sheet: A financial statement issued by corporations indicating company assets, liabilities and shareholder equity.

Basis: The cost of an asset for calculating gain or loss. Required for tax purposes. The basis will be the cost of the security plus commissions.

Bear Market: A declining market with depressed stock prices.

Bills: Government short term securities of 13, 26 and 52 week maturities.

Blue chip stock: Shares of a large, profitable well known companies that consistently experience steady growth, dividends and profits.

Bond: A long term debt obligation , government or industry, that is issued at a set interest rate for a predetermined number of years. The security for a bond is often a mortgage.

Book value: Total company assets less

total debt divided by common shares outstanding. Preferred stock is considered a company debt. The book value is the value per share of company stock that would revert to the shareholder if the company liquidated assets and terminated business activities.

Broker: The intermediary agent that buys and sells securities and real property to a second party for a commission.

Bullion: Precious metals such as gold and silver. Sold by weight in bars and minted coins.

Bull Market: A rising market with stock prices increasing.

Capital Gains or (losses): The profit or (loss) resulting from the sale of stock. The difference between the purchase and sales price of your securities.

Capitalization: A companies total security (stock) market value.

Certificate of deposit (CD): A financial institutions redeemable debt instrument. If purchased from a bank or Savings and loan most are guaranteed for up to $100.000 by the U.S. Government. Check for FDIC insured at local banks.

Commercial paper: A short term debt security issued by solid companies usually for under 270 days. Money market accounts invest heavily in short term paper.

Depreciation: Value reduction of

Depreciation: Value reduction of equipment or realestate. Real property value decreases over time. A major computer system that costs several thousand dollars will be worth less after a years use. This reduced value is deductible. Rental property also depreciates.

Diversification: Reduce investment risk by purchasing stocks from different industries, bonds, mutual funds and other securities. Prevents major capital loss if one investment fails.

Dividend: The amount a company pays per share to each shareholder of record. Not all companies pay dividends. If a company currently pays $1.00 per share the payout is often quarterly and would be 25 cents per quarter.

Dollar cost averaging: Purchasing a fixed dollar amount of a security each month no matter what the market condition is. Often fractions of shares are purchased in dividend reinvestment plans. The cost of all shares purchased average over time.

Earnings per share (EPS): The net income divided by the outstanding shares of a company. Preferred stock dividends are first subtracted from the net before calculations are made.

Equity: A companies value, equity per share, after subtracting liabilities. Assets minus liabilities.

Ex-dividend date: The date dividends

Executor: The individual selected to execute a will.

Face Value: The stated value printed on the face of a bond. The face amount is paid back to the bond holder at maturity. Often referred to as par value.

Financial statement: An audited accounting statement of a companies assets and liabilities.

Fiscal year: Firms can choose to follow an operational cycle rather than a calendar year. The Federal government has a fiscal year that starts on October 1 and ends on Sept. 30th.

Fundamental analysis: An analysis and evaluation of a firms financial position, managerial strengths and earnings.

Gross income: Total income from all sources before taxes.

Growth stock: A company with rapid earnings growth. Often have above average risk and high P/E ratios.

High flyers: Stocks with abnormally high price movements. Takeover candidates often experience excessive price increases on takeover rumors. If the deal falls through the prices tumble.

Holding company: A company that has controling interest, through stock ownership, of other company.

controling interest, through stock ownership, of other company.

Index fund: Mutual funds that attempt to match the performance of one of the popular indexes, DJIA, S&P, etc., by investing in the index's stock listings.

Individual retirement account (IRA): Long term pension savings plans that earn tax deferred interest and can reduce your taxable income.

Interest: Payments to a lender for the use of their money.

Liability: The debt or obligations of a company.

Load: Sales charge or commission paid to mutual fund above the funds net asset value. Over 300 funds do not charge a sales load.

Margin: Qualified investors can purchase stock on margin. They can finance a large portion of the investment from the broker and pay interest on the margin loan. Big investors can borrow up to 50% of the purchase price of a stock transaction. (very risky).

Market indexes: The Dow Jones Industrial Average, S & P 500, The New York Times, New York Exchange and AMEX all have their own index. The dow is comprised of 30 leading companies. The total market value of the companies are tabulated and a divisor is established to provide a trackable index figure. A change in the index number indicates a gain or loss of total capitalization securities market. Financial institutions that buy, sell and transfer short term commercial paper, Treasury bills, CD's and short term tax-exempt notes.

Mortgage: The person that lends money to a second party to purchase property has a claim on the property until the loan is paid off. The claim on the property is the mortgage and protects the lender if the loan is not repaid.

Mutual fund: A professionally managed investment company that pools investors cash to purchase stocks, bonds and Treasury notes to earn income for share holders.

NASDAQ: The National Association of Securities Dealers Automated Quotations. A system providing brokers with price quotes for stocks traded on the OTC, over-the-counter, market.

NAV: Net asset value; A mutual funds per share value. The NAV is calculated by adding up the market value of all securities owned by the fund and dividing the total value by the shares outstanding. The NAV changes daily.

No-load fund: A mutual fund that sells direct to the public and does not charge a sales commission.

NYSE: The New York Stock Exchange; One of the worlds largest stock / investment trading markets. Began in 1792 and was named the New York Stock Exchange in 1817. In 1827 only 31 companies were listed on the exchange.

trading markets. Began in 1792 and was named the New York Stock Exchange in 1817. In 1827 only 31 companies were listed on the exchange.

Odd lot: Stock transactions of less than 100 shares, one round lot. Odd lot purchases are assessed an additional odd lot transaction fee added to the standard commission charge.

Open-end fund: A mutual fund that issues new shares for each new buyer.

Over-the-counter: The direct selling and buying of securities through dealers. Many of the transactions are made by phone instead of on an exchange floor.

Penny stocks: Speculative, low priced, high risk stocks trading for less than one dollar. Today stocks under five dollars per share are considered penny stocks. These high risk investment should be avoided by new investors.

Portfolio: The stocks, bonds and other securities owned by an individual. To avoid undue risk a diversified portfolio is recommended.

Preferred stock: Issued by companies like common stock but with additional benefits. Generally pay higher dividends than the common stock and if a company liquidates preferred stock owners have first rights to company assets after the creditors are paid. Usually preferred stock does not have voting rights.

Principal: The face amount of a bond. The part of the mortgage payment that is

Commission from companies issuing new securities. Mutual funds will send out a prospectus upon request.

Real return: An investments return after adjusting for inflation.

REIT: Real-estate investment trust; Similar to an investment company but primarily invests in real estate. REIT's often distribute up to 90% of their income to share holders.

Rollover: Placing IRA or other retirement plan assets into another investment vehicle.

Round lot: A stock transaction of 100 shares.

S & P: Standard & Poor's Corporation. A company that specialized in market statistics and stock and bond analysis. Developed one of the primary stock market indexes, the S & P 500.

SEC: Security and Exchange Commission; A federal agency that regulates the securities industry.

Securities: A legal document which proves ownership or claims something of value. Examples are stocks, bonds, commodity contracts,etc..

Speculating: Investing funds in high risk securities to achieve extremely high returns.

Spread: The difference between the buy and sell price of a stock or mutual fund.

Spread: The difference between the buy and sell price of a stock or mutual fund.

Stock split: The division of a companies stock into a greater number of shares. A 2 for 1 split would give each shareholder one additional share for each share held. If a company had 2,000,000 share outstanding before the split they would now have 4,000,000 shares outstanding. Share price generally decreases when the stock splits. Reverse splits are also possible.

Tax shelter: Investments that reduce taxable income resulting in a tax savings for the year.

Technical analysis: Stock analysis based on historical price, earnings and trading volume.

Trader: An investor that buys and sells to realize short term profits.

Transfer agent: The person who records each registered shareholders name address and number of shares owned.

Trust: When one person (trustee) holds property that benefits another.

Volume: The total shares traded on any given day for a particular issue or total of all transactions on a given exchange.

Yield: An investments return expressed as a percentage of current price.

APPENDIX

Resources

Books

Market Fundamentals

Many of the books listed can be found in your library. Check your library's card file to locate additional sources.

Why Stocks Go Up (and Down), by William H. Pike, Richard D. Irwin, 1818 Ridge Rd., Homewood, Il 60430.

Fundamentals of the Securities Industry-Revised Edition, by Allan H. Pessin, Prentice-Hall, Box 500, Englewood Cliffs, NJ 07632.

Gaining on the Market, by Charles J. Rolo, Atlantic-Little, Brown, 34 Beacon St., Boston, MA 02108

Stock Market Blueprints, by Edward S. Jensen. This book can be requested free of charge when opening an account with Quick & Reilly, Inc. An excellent reference text.

The New York Times Complete Guide to Personal Investing, by Gary L Klott.

Bonds

How to Invest in Bonds, by Hugh C. Sherwood, Walker & Co., 720 Fifth Ave., New York, NY 10019.

The complete Bond Book, by David M. Darst, McGraw-Hill, 1221 Avenue of the Americas, New York, NY 10020.

The Handbook of Fixed Income Securities, edited by Frank J. Fabozzi and Irving m. Pollack, Richard D. Irwin, 1818 Ridge Road, Homewood, Il. 60430.

Banking and Financial Planning

The Only Money Book for the Middle Class, by Don and Joan German. William Morrow & Co., 105 Madison Ave., New York, NY 10016.

Money A to Z: A Consumer's Guide to the language of Personal Finance, by Don and Joan German, Facts on File, 460 Park Ave.S., New York, NY 10016.

Be Your Own Financial Planner, by Dorlene V. Shane.

Mutual Funds

The New Mutual Fund Investment Advisor, by Richard Dorf.

The Individual Investor's Guide to No-Load Mutual Funds, The American Association of Individual Investors, 612 North Michigan Avenue, Dept. NLG, Chicago, IL 60611.

Successful Investing in Mutual Funds, by Alan Pope, John Wiley & Sons, 605 Third Avenue, New York, NY 10158

The Guild to Mutual Funds, The Investment Company Institute, 1600 M Street NW, Washington, DC 20036.

Financial Courses

The Money Course, A 300 page personal financial management course, by Money Magazine, c/o Time Education Center, 10 North Main Street, Yardley, PA 19067-9986. Sells for $79.95.

NAIC Stock Study Course, National Association of Investors Corporation, 1515 E. Eleven Mile Road, Royal Oak, Michigan 48067. Members can purchase this course for $60.00.

Magazines

MONEY Magazine, on most news stands.

Money Maker, a one year subscription comes with a 354 page Guide to Successful Investing. Subscription costs $13.98 for one year and can be ordered from Money Maker, Dept. HAB7, P.O. Box 3084, Harlan, IA 51593-0148.

Better Investing Magazine, Published by The National Association of Investors Corporation, 1515 E. Eleven Mile Road, Royal Oak, Michigan 48067. Subscription rate $17.00 or for $31 per year you can become a member of the association and receive their investment guide, magazine and other membership benefits.

Sylvia Porter's Personal Finance Magazine, on most news stands.

There are many other financial/business magazines available. The above four prove excellent reading for the beginning investor.

INDEX

ORDER FORM

D-Amp Publications
401-B Amherst Avenue
Coraopolis, PA 15108

Please send me the following books and reports by Dennis Damp.

Dollars and Sense	$12.95
Government Employment Guide (A guide for those interested in obtaining a Federal job. Presented in a workbook format.)	$ 9.95
(Report T-1) The one-time tax exclusion that allows home sellers who are 55 or over to keep up to $125,000 of resale profits tax free. Look before you leap. By not planning this tax break carefully you could lose thousands in taxes.	$ 6.95

AMORTIZATION SCHEDULES (each) $30.00
See chapter 8 for details. Must specify mortgage amount, Interest rate, Date first payment was due, and mortgage term.

Name: ______________________________
Address: ___________________________
____
______________________________ Zip: ______

Pennsylvania residents add 6% sales tax.
SHIPPING: Add $1.00 shipping for each item ordered.